T. L. Shore

D0866511

A Wife's Purpose

A Wife's Purpose

Cindy
Schaap

SWORD of the LORD
PUBLISHERS
P. O. BOX 1099, MURFREESBORO, TN 37133

Copyright 1992 by
SWORD OF THE LORD PUBLISHERS
ISBN 0-87398-944-9

Second Printing: 1993

Printed and Bound in the United States of America

Dedication

". . . because I have you in my heart . . ."
(Philippians 1:7)

This book is dedicated to

• My husband, Jack Schaap. He exemplifies Ephesians 5:25. *"Husbands, love your wives, even as Christ also loved the church, and gave himself for it."* Through knowing him, I better understand how much God loves me. He is my hero as a Christian.

• My dad, Dr. Jack Hyles. He was my first love, and he nurtured that love with Christ-likeness and care. My buddy, as I called him, will always hold a special place in my heart. As my pastor, he has taught me more about how to live a joyful Christian life than anyone. I wish everyone could sit under his preaching.

• My mom, Beverly Hyles. By always being there, sometimes in the shadows, she taught me what being a good wife and mother is really about.

• All three of you. You are my favorite people and have shown a commitment to Christ regardless of the cost.

Table of Contents

Foreword

". . . a prudent wife is from the Lord."
(Proverbs 19:14)

In 1976, when I was 17 years old, I was attending a national conference on revival and soul winning with my parents in Atlanta, Georgia. At that conference, I heard a 50-year-old preacher from Hammond, Indiana, tell how he traveled the country 50 weeks out of every year. He told how he said good-bye to his family at the breakfast table on Monday morning and did not see them again until after the midweek service at his church on Wednesday evening.

He mentioned in the sermon that he had two single daughters living at home. At the mention of two single daughters, my 17-year-old antenna began to tune in more closely to his sermon. He mentioned that the youngest of his daughters, 16-year-old Cindy, would wait for him after the midweek service while he counseled many of his church members until late in the evening. He said when he opened his door to leave for home, this daughter would run to his side and snuggle up close as they walked down the hallway. "She's a snuggler, not a hugger," he said. At the sound of a snuggling girl about my age, my antenna went up much higher and tuned in to this man's frequency much more closely. He went on to say that this 16-year-old, single, snuggling daughter of his would ask him the same question every week: "Did you get any preacher boys on fire for God this week, Daddy?" At that point, this preacher had my fullest attention as those were the three things I was looking for in a young lady: a spiritual, single, snuggling girl – although not necessarily in that order!

At that moment, something inside told me I was going to meet that girl. The problem was that she was living in northwest Indiana and I was attending college in Minnesota.

Four months later, I was sitting in the office of my new pastor during Christmas break from college. This new pastor just happened to be a graduate of Hyles-Anderson College – located in **northwest Indiana**. The chancellor of that college just happened to be that 50-year-old preacher who had a single, snuggling, spiritual daughter. My new pastor told me he felt God would have me transfer to Hyles-Anderson College and finish my education there. Thirty days later, I was enrolled as a student at Hyles-Anderson College.

During my first week at this new college, I was approached by a lady on a Wednesday evening in the auditorium of First Baptist Church of Hammond. This lady in her fifties, who had been a member of First Baptist Church for most of her life, just happened to be the mother-in-law of the new pastor at my home church. Of course, I knew none of this as she approached me.

Only she and I were in that vast auditorium that seats well over 6,000 people. She marched right up to me and said, "I know who you are; you are Jack Schaap. **And** I know who you are going to marry." Before I could think of an appropriate response to this unusual statement, she continued, "You are going to marry the preacher's daughter, Cindy Hyles."

Stunned by this amazing prophecy, I found my ride home and went back to the dormitories where I sat on the edge of my bunk bed rethinking the evening's events.

At that moment, one of my roommates came into our room, walked up to the bed, and said, "Jack, I have a girl in mind I think you ought to consider dating."

I quickly responded, "I sure hope she's the same one I'm supposed to marry."

He shot back, "Are you engaged to be married?"

I quickly replied, "No, but tonight at church someone told me she knew who I was going to marry." My roommate tried to find out who this might be, but I was too embarrassed to tell him what this unusual lady had informed me that evening. I said, "You'd laugh at me if I told you what she said tonight, but please do tell me whom you think I should date."

My roommate said, "I think you should seriously consider dating Cindy Hyles, the preacher's daughter."

I couldn't believe my ears. I felt there surely must be some conspiracy afoot trying to get me to meet and date this Cindy Hyles girl. Of course, my mind immediately shot back to August of the previous year when I had heard about this girl and felt something inside tell me I was going to meet her someday. My curiosity was quickly becoming overwhelming.

About one month later, my parents were visiting me at college, and we were standing in the foyer of First Baptist Church when Cindy Hyles walked by us with some of her friends. (At that time, Cindy and I had not met or been introduced, but I did know who she was.) My mother grabbed my arm and said as she pointed at Cindy, "Who is that girl right there?" I responded that she was the preacher's daughter, Cindy Hyles. My mother quickly said, "That is the girl I have been praying for you to meet and marry for more than 19 years."

A few weeks after that conversation, I was introduced to Cindy, and she and I began dating. Immediately, I had the assurance from my parents and the Holy Spirit that this was the girl I was going to marry. Later, I found out that she had the same assurance as quickly as I did.

Both of our parents seemed to know from the very

beginning that we had each found our lifelong mate and began to counsel us and express their confidence that we were doing the right thing.

Of course, with all the strange events that led to my meeting Cindy, I needed no one's prodding to convince me this was most certainly the girl I was destined to marry. In fact, I fell in love immediately and needed only much patience to wait for the right time to ask her to marry me.

Eight months after our first date, I called Cindy's dad long distance and asked him if I could ask Cindy to marry me. He at once asked me to meet him in his office as soon as I could drive down from Michigan.

Several hours later, I was sitting in his office, and he explained to me that he would give us his blessing and permission to marry if we so chose. He also said Cindy would make a very good wife for me. Of course, I was thrilled with his permission and a good wife was exactly what I wanted!

However, he continued by saying that if we would wait one year longer and give him time to groom and polish her, that he could insure that Cindy would not be just a **good** wife—rather, she would be a **great** wife. Well, how could I turn down a great wife over a good wife?

Cindy and I have been married now for more than twelve years. I can honestly say that I have received a great wife. In Proverbs 19:14, God says that *"a prudent wife is from the Lord."* A synonym for the word *prudent* could be *matched, fitted,* or *appropriate.* Cindy is my perfect match, and she is very fitted and suitable for me.

I have personally experienced and witnessed two marriages that I felt were the ideals of what God intended marriage to be. One is the marriage of my parents, and the other is the marriage I enjoy with Cindy.

I am not saying sweet things about my wife because a husband is expected to do so for his wife's first book. Not everything comes easily or naturally for my wife. Time and time again, her left-handedness has been an occasion for awkwardness as she grew up in a right-handed world. Cindy has no unique talents that would cause her to stand out from any other Christian lady. The strength of my wife is her unwavering commitment to a standard of excellence in every area of life. This commitment has forged a character and discipline that I could only wish every Christian wife would emulate and the kind of godly maturity and affectionate love in marriage that I could only wish every Christian husband could know in his wife.

The pages in this book are not the writings of an armchair philosopher. These are the writings hammered out in Cindy's mind and heart while on her knees before God in prayer, while at her desk diligently studying God's Word by the hour, and tried and proven on the practical day-by-day playing field of marriage, child rearing, and life with a very busy and demanding husband.

Any Christian wife would do well to emulate the example and teachings of this book and to study and emulate the life of the author.

— *Jack Schaap*

Acknowledgements

*"And whatsoever ye do in word or deed, do all
in the name of the Lord Jesus, giving thanks to
God and the Father by him." (Colossians 3:17)*

I would like to express my thanks to Linda
Stubblefield who was the one person I needed to hear say,
"You can do it!" I also would like to thank Linda
Stubblefield, Kelly Sikma, Angie Zachary, and Dr. Viola
Walden for their help in typesetting and proofreading.
These ladies have taught me to appreciate the word *servant*
more. *"But he that is greatest among you shall be your
servant."* (Matthew 23:11)

I must thank my husband's parents, Ken and
Marlene Schaap, for devoting much of their time and talent
to the rearing of a little boy who would grow to be a
wonderful husband. He's been God's greatest gift, and I
owe them a great debt.

I must also thank the members of First Baptist
Church of Hammond, Indiana, for committing themselves
to a man, his cause, and his family the same year that I was
born. They have prayed for me and loved me. Most of all,
they have taught me thousands of things just by their
example. They are the greatest Christians in the world, and
I love them.

I thank the Hyles-Anderson College preachers' wives whom it has been my privilege to teach the past seven years. I have taught them biblical principles for a happy marriage. They have taught me by their love and sacrifice.

I thank my siblings, Becky, David, and Linda. Being the youngest in our family, I have learned through their successes and disappointments. I thank them for going before me. They will always be my personal heroes.

I would like to acknowledge my aunt, Mrs. Earlyne Stephens, for contributing the chapter entitled, "Financial Bliss." I admire her wisdom in handling the finances as Bursar at Hyles-Anderson College. I also admire her sweetness as a Christian lady. She is unsurpassed in both areas.

My grandmother, Mrs. C. M. Slaughter, went to Heaven during the writing of this book. I am thankful for what she and her husband left me. I would like to acknowledge my grandmother, Mrs. Coystal Hyles, who is in Heaven. She gave her all to the Lord in spite of much adversity and provided for me the root of my heritage.

Introduction

"And Jesus was called . . . to the marriage."
(John 2:2)

At the time of this writing, I have been teaching a class on the subject of marriage for approximately seven years. While studying for and teaching this class, I have become acquainted with some philosophies that have been a real help to my marriage. I consider it a privilege to share these philosophies with my students at Hyles-Anderson College and with you as a reader. I am confident that the principles taught in this book have the potential to be helpful to the average reader. However, I realize that there are some marriage problems that are not textbook in their fashion. Therefore, I want to emphasize that this book is not meant to be a condemnation of those who experience unhappy marriages. I also want to remind you that there are problems that can best be corrected by personal counseling. I would recommend counseling with the pastor of a local New Testament church.

I am aware that the current divorce rate in the United States is somewhere around 50 percent. I wish to remind you, however, that marriage is a God-ordained institution. Therefore, marriage is excellent and cannot fail. When we hear of a marriage that has ended in divorce, we must remember that it is not the marriage that has failed; it is the people who have failed. Because of this, I believe a person can come from a family where literally every other member is divorced, yet still have the same potential for a happy home as does someone who comes from a family of well-adjusted marriages. The former person may have to catch up on her preparation, but her marriage can succeed. When two people commit themselves to following the marriage principles prescribed in the Bible, there is always hope.

Not only is marriage a God-ordained institution, but it is also the **first** God-ordained institution. I therefore believe that marriage is the most powerful relationship in the world. In other words, when two people who are committed to God become as "one flesh," their power increases perhaps a thousand-fold. The liability to this power is that it challenges the devil to attack the home more than any other institution. I think the reason for this attack is that he knows how important this foundational institution is to our society. In fact, I feel that almost every problem we wrestle with in society today can be traced back to the crumbling of America's homes. For this reason and others, the Lord has given me what I believe is an unusual burden for the marriages of our Christian families. It saddens me when anyone takes lightly the calling and preparation of the Christian wife.

I have often heard people say at baby showers what a solemn responsibility it is when one becomes a parent. God entrusts a new parent with an eternal soul. Yet I believe that when I became a wife, God also entrusted me with an eternal soul. That is not to say that my husband belongs to me. Rather, he is a possession of God's whom God has entrusted to me. God trusts that I will take care of him to the best of my ability and in light of my husband's eternal purpose in God's scheme of things.

First Thessalonians 5:24 says, *"Faithful is he that calleth you, who also will do it."* In spite of my wonderful upbringing, I must say that I was a pretty independent and rebellious individual when I submitted to the call to become

Mrs. Jack Schaap. However, God has been faithful, and when He called me to be a wife, He also began to tenderly and gently give me the ability to meet my husband's needs and to experience a harmonious marriage relationship. The wonderful fact is that the ability given to me is available to every Christian lady who is willing to seek out the wisdom of God. Therefore, I gladly share with you what I believe is the purpose of the Christian wife.

It is with great fear and trembling that I have written a book on the subject of marriage. As a preacher's daughter, I well understand that a speaker's or a writer's message will be tested. Because of this fact, I deeply appreciate my husband's allowing me to write this book.

I have not written this book because I am the wife best qualified, but because I felt this was what God wanted me to do. It is not my wish that this book will cause you to be too introspective, but that you will use it only as you see a need. My ultimate wish is that it will encourage each of us to love our husbands more. If it does not accomplish this mission, then I have failed. Thank you for sharing this book with me.

Cindy Schaap
I Samuel 12:24

"Only fear the Lord,
and serve him in truth with all your heart:
for consider how great things he hath done for you."

God's so good to give us purpose;
A work which we were made to do.
He could have done it all without us,
But in His sovereign mind He knew
We would need a task to greet us
To help us face another day.
We would need to know when dying
The work we've done won't pass away.
God's so good to give us purpose;
A work which we were made to do.
In His sovereign mind He planned it.
My purpose would be loving you.

CHAPTER I

A Wife's Purpose

"And the Lord God said, It is not good that the man should be alone; I will make him an help meet for him." (Genesis 2:18)

When a woman becomes a wife, her very purpose for existence becomes that of fulfilling the needs and satisfying the desires of her husband—the man with whom she has become one flesh. God does not give us this purpose because in His male image He delights in making women inferior. God in His foreknowledge knew there would always be only one thing that would fully satisfy a wife. He knew that thing would be satisfying the needs of the husband God provided for her. Because God designed it to be so, a wife will be frustrated if she tries to find her primary fulfillment in any other avenue.

When a bride-to-be thinks of being a helpmeet to her future husband, it may sound easy. However, the wife of two or three years discovers that her task is rather complicated. It is complicated because a man has many types of needs which need to be met. Those needs can be broken down into four categories:

- physical needs
- social needs
- intellectual needs
- spiritual needs

Many wives meet their husband's physical needs—even those whose marriages are unhappy. These wives cook their husband's meals, care for his clothing, and provide a clean and comfortable atmosphere for him.

Fewer women care enough to meet the social and intellectual needs of their husbands. Many married women would try to meet these needs by sharing their time with their husbands, especially in an activity he would enjoy. They also would meet his intellectual needs by communicating with him in ways that would interest him.

However, very few are the women who meet their husband's spiritual needs—his eternal needs. This is sad for three reasons:

- An eternal God would certainly be most interested in His men having their spiritual needs met.
- A man who has no spiritual counterpart will certainly have a more difficult time accomplishing his eternal purpose.
- A woman will surely be frustrated when she does not practice the highest form of her spiritual calling.

Let me summarize then what I believe is a wife's purpose (her highest calling). **A wife's purpose is to meet her husband's spiritual needs by helping him do the things God made him to do, or a wife's purpose is to help her husband realize his fullest spiritual potential.** I can testify that this is the most satisfying, yet the most difficult, aspect of marriage.

God has given me several responsibilities other than being a helpmeet to Jack. I am the mother of two children, a daughter Jaclynn, age 10; and a son Kenny, age 7. I thoroughly enjoy being their mother. I am a Sunday school teacher to fifth-grade girls. I am a college teacher and have been for seven years. I enjoy writing and sometimes traveling and speaking to groups of ladies. However, none of the things mentioned is my highest calling, nor do they bring me my greatest fulfillment. My greatest fulfillment comes when I see my husband being used to affect the lives of other people and realize that I had a part in it.

I strive to the best of my ability to maintain a clean, comfortable home for my husband. I cook nutritious meals for him and care for his physical needs. However, this is not the highest aspect of my calling. Why? Because these are all merely temporal things, and I am an eternal being with an eternal calling. My Christian husband is a spiritual being who has an eternal soul and who must stand before God someday.

Again, my highest calling is to meet my husband's spiritual needs, and nothing can satisfy quite like it. When I try to find my fulfillment using any other thing as a substitute, I will be frustrated and will not know the complete satisfaction that God planned for me to have. This generation is a generation of a 50-percent divorce rate and frustrated women.

Do spiritual needs exist only for those husbands called into the ministry? Certainly not! God has an eternal purpose for every person He creates. Let me illustrate. My husband's secretary, Barbara Burke, is a lady whom I admire tremendously. Though she does a wonderful job as a secretary, she often makes it evident to me that she has not forgotten her purpose. For example, above her typewriter in her office, she keeps a deacons' list posted. Underlined on that list are the words *Paul Burke – deacon.* I would guess that Barbara uses this as a prayer reminder and also as a reminder of her purpose. I have no doubt that Barbara's husband Paul has reached his fullest spiritual potential and will continue to grow. I am sure that this is not only because of his own desires and abilities, but also because of the help of his spiritual counterpart. It is exciting and fulfilling to watch our husbands' potential grow.

I believe the first sin in the Bible could have been avoided if Eve had remembered her purpose of meeting her husband's spiritual needs. Imagine what would have happened if Eve had asked herself the question, "Will taking a bite of this fruit help Adam spiritually or will it hinder him?" However, Eve was not thinking about her purpose. She was thinking about the one thing she did not have.

Perfect Fellowship

Have you ever considered how wonderful Eve's circumstances were? She lived in the beautiful Garden of Eden. The most beautiful place I have ever visited is a little island called Little Stirrup Cay. When my husband and I were approaching our tenth wedding anniversary, he suggested that we take a special trip to celebrate. I suggested to him that he go by himself to the travel agency, plan the trip, and surprise me. A few days later, he came home with several brochures and informed me that we were scheduled to take a cruise to the Bahamas. I was devastated. I had never had any desire to be on a ship in the middle of a big ocean. However, as the time for our departure approached, I became very excited.

On one day of that glorious week in the Bahamas, we went to a small island that was owned by the cruise line with which we were traveling. The island was the closest thing to being primitive that I have ever seen. The only people on that island were from our ship. No one actually resided there. My husband and I spent the day miles away from anyone, resting on a hammock strung between two palm trees less than ten feet from the ocean. It was really a "rough" day. I cannot think of any place that could have been more beautiful, but I'm sure the home of God's first creation was beautiful beyond compare.

Eve must have been the most beautiful woman who has ever existed. Can you imagine being created by God on sight? Now I was created by God also, but my mother and father interfered and left me with some less than desirable characteristics (as well as some pretty good ones, I might add!). Eve's husband must have been handsome because he was created on sight by God also. I would picture him as a dark-haired man because my husband has dark hair. Some readers may picture him as blond, gray-haired, or maybe even bald. I am not sure what he looked like, but I do imagine that he was handsome.

I would tend to believe that Adam and Eve had an excellent relationship. They were perfectly matched by God Himself. I'm sure many single young people have wished they could find a life's mate in that way.

The greatest thing is that they had perfect fellowship with God. Imagine what it must have been like to talk with God and to hear His voice speaking back to you. There have been some times in my life when I would have given anything to be able to hear God's voice as I asked the question, "Why?" Eve was in exactly that type of situation; nevertheless, she was dissatisfied. Why? The devil caused her to think about the one thing she wanted that she could not have.

The devil has no new tricks, and this is still the way he causes women to forget their purpose today. He puts their minds upon wanting things (such as home furnishings, clothes, and vacations) that they do not have. The way the devil gets to a man is through the dissatisfaction of a woman.

- The devil most often destroys a man through a woman.
- The devil most often destroys a woman through dissatisfaction.

Have you ever wondered why God attributes the first sin in the Bible to a man instead of to a woman? *"Wherefore, as by one man sin entered into the world, and death by sin; and so death passed upon all men, for that all have sinned."* (Romans 5:12) Was it not Eve who first took of the forbidden fruit? My dad and pastor, Dr. Jack Hyles explains it this way. Because women are emotional beings, they are more easily deceived. Therefore, it is my dad's belief that Eve partook of the fruit because she was deceived. She honestly did not believe she would lose eternal life. She believed the devil instead of God. However, Adam, being a much less emotional creature, knew full well that he would lose eternal life. He stubbornly took the fruit anyway. Why? Because he wanted to please his wife.

A man has a strong and natural desire to please his wife. He may not show it by succumbing to her desires every time she nags him. He may not even manifest any concern or compassion when she nags. He may not outwardly say, "Honey, I have a tremendous desire to please you, so of course I would love to take the garbage out more often." However, his desire to please is still part of his nature as a man. He desires to hear the praise and see the admiration of his wife. Therefore, a man will generally do one of two things when his wife is constantly dissatisfied:

- He will leave her either physically or emotionally.
- After a long period of holding out, he will change to her way of thinking.

How does the devil use a woman to hinder a man spiritually? He causes her to lose sight of her purpose of helping her husband find and do God's will. It is only natural that a woman is more interested in material things because she is in charge of clothing and feeding her family and maintaining a comfortable home for them. Her desire to do these things and to do them well is not in itself unspiritual. It is when she takes material things out of their proper priority and makes them her purpose that she becomes worldly and ungodly.

A man who is seeking to do God's will and who has an uninterested wife **may** continue to do God's will in spite of his wife. (I would certainly hope that no person would have to say that they did anything good in **spite** of me.) He may leave her behind emotionally and pursue his spiritual purpose on his own. However, it takes a very strong man to do this, and he will accomplish much less on his own than he could have with his intended spiritual counterpart.

A weaker man will eventually come around to his wife's way of thinking and become most interested in material things himself. Therefore, he will either decrease his service for Christ, or he will not do much of anything for Christ. I'm afraid that too often the latter is true. When a man does something, he either puts his whole heart into it or his whole heart out of it. A wife usually doesn't intend for her husband to leave God's will completely. She intends for him to put in his little bit of service. She just doesn't want him to be fanatical about it—at least not so fanatical that he causes her any material discomfort. Unfortunately, the wife is the loser in this situation as she will never have the satisfaction that comes only by fulfilling her God-given purpose as a married woman.

Then if a wife is to fulfill her God-given purpose by serving as her husband's spiritual counterpart, how can she accomplish this without becoming his nag and worst critic?

First, let us establish the fact that nagging is not the answer. If it worked, I would highly recommend it because it is a very easy tool to use. All a wife has to do is to open her mouth and wag her tongue. It is an easy, uncreative, and unsuccessful method of bringing about change in people. Many people think of nagging as harsh words said in a very unkind, maybe even violent manner. I take this definition one step further. I believe nagging is this and more.

I have been brought up with the training that it is wrong to use cruel words and violence to bring about change in a person, especially one's husband. Therefore, avoiding these things has not been difficult in my marriage. That does not mean I don't think of a lot of other equally damaging ways to nag Jack. My nagging usually comes in the form of "well-meant suggestions," namely, using kind words in a kind manner to belittle him and to get him to see things my way. Therefore, I have coined my definition of nagging.

Nagging is making a well-meant suggestion
outside one's own realm of authority.

For example, if my husband comes into my kitchen and makes suggestions about how I could better organize my kitchen cabinets, I will feel offended and belittled. No matter how kindly his expression or tone of voice and no matter how hard I try to be understanding, I will feel that a certain amount of criticism has been directed my way. Why? Because he has made a well-meant suggestion which is outside his realm. Though a husband is biblically the head of the wife, it is my belief that the marriage will work better if the husband gives his wife her own realm of authority and then allows her to "rule" in that realm any way she chooses.

The same thing would happen if I should make well-meant suggestions about my husband's work at the office, his personal habits, etc. These things are a part of his own dominion, and no matter how well I phrase my complaints, my suggestions will be threatening.

You may be wondering how you can possibly be a help to your husband and his spiritual potential if you are unable to make even one "lousy" suggestion about anything that is in his realm. Let me share with you a formula for completing your husband versus changing him.

Changing = Nagging + Criticism
Completing = Prayer + Praise + Action

When we are trying to change our husbands, we willfully make them the way we wish them to be. We will use nagging and criticism, and, as we've established previously, these simply do not work. When we are trying to complete them, we give the best of ourselves to compliment that which is best about our husbands. We use prayer, praise, and action to accent their strengths, not erase the weaknesses.

Let's say a young bride is having a problem with a husband who simply cannot get out of bed and get to work on time in the morning. She sees that problems are about to result. Of course, she feels insecure about this. A wife finds security in her husband, and his weaknesses cause her to feel insecure. So, her natural impulse is to nag and to criticize when she sees weakness in his life. Therefore, when he sleeps in, she may roll over in bed and remind him to get up. When this reminder doesn't work, she may give him a full-fledged lecture complete with lots of suggestions. Her promptings belittle him, question his ability to be any kind of success in life, and maybe even contain a few comparisons with other men. Classically, the wife may then roll over and go back to sleep.

Because she has backed her husband into a corner by tearing his opinion of himself to shreds, his response probably will be to retaliate with some nagging and criticizing of his own. After this, she may end the conversation by saying, "I don't know why you get so upset. I was only trying to help." Hopefully, the conversation will end there, and more unkind words will be left unsaid. Still, a husband is left with much unresolved bitterness in his heart, and his sweetheart, the one with whom he could not wait to spend time every day, has become more like a mother to him. She has become the last one with whom he wants to spend time and the greatest destroyer of his self-esteem. Alienation is always the result of nagging.

Nagging changes the sweetheart relationship into a mother-son relationship. I am fond of the mother-son relationship. I have a son who, at the time of this writing, is six years old, and I enjoy our relationship very much. However, my romantic nature causes me to need to be somebody's sweetheart. You don't have to observe the marriages of the world to see the effects of nagging. I think I would be willing to sacrifice a few things to preserve my sweetheart relationship.

On the other hand, let's suppose this young bride we have been talking about decides to complete her husband by using prayer, praise, and action. Let's see how she could put these valuable methods to use.

Prayer, Praise, and Action Methods

1. Prayer. The young bride would come to the Lord asking Him to help her husband with his problem of oversleeping. **She would ask the Lord to give her ideas of things she could do to help him with his problem. She also would ask the Lord to give her an attitude of acceptance rather than change.** In any situation, a spouse should realize that her perception of the problem could be false. In other words, she must realize that she is not always right. Also, she should leave her spouse's weakness with the Lord and spend time other than prayer time thinking about her husband's strengths rather than his weaknesses.

2. Praise. She would look for times when she could sincerely praise her husband for the **opposite quality.** That is, when she sees him performing in a manner that is the opposite of his particular weakness, she can point out his positive behavior to him through praise. This praise paints a picture for her husband, allowing him to see himself as doing right in his area of weakness. *"As the fining pot for silver, and the furnace for gold; so is a man to his praise."* (Proverbs 27:21)

Praise is a key to a happy marital relationship. I will

devote an entire chapter to it later in this book. Praise paints a picture of ourselves, and we as human beings tend to act out the picture that has been painted for us by the praise or criticism of others.

3. Action. She would list things that she herself could do to make it easier for her husband to do right **on his own** concerning this weakness.

> • She could get out of bed some time before her husband needs to be awakened and plan her schedule of rest accordingly.
> • She **should** have herself looking pretty before her husband needs to be up each morning.
> • She could bring a favorite drink to his bedside as his alarm goes off each morning. (Breakfast in bed each morning would also be a good alternative, but I'm afraid quite unrealistic.)
> • She could start some cheerful (not irritating) music when the alarm goes off each morning.
> • She could **offer** to set out his clothes in the morning, get his bath or shower ready, etc.

The point is that after the wife uses prayer, praise, and action to help her husband, he is going to feel better about himself even while one of his problems is being corrected. An important concept to remember in understanding human relations is that, in any situation, we can either tear down or build up the lives of others. A wife never has to tear down her husband. Proverbs 14:1 says, *"Every wise woman buildeth her house: but the foolish plucketh it down with her hands."*

To complete a husband takes quite a bit more work than nagging or criticizing. Yet if a wife wants to be a spiritual counterpart to him, she must not only meet his physical, mental, and social needs, but also his spiritual needs. If she wants to see him reach his fullest spiritual potential and she wants to feel completely satisfied, she must remember the formula:

Completing = Prayer + Praise + Action

Now that we've discussed our formula, let me give you some more ideas about how to help your husband reach his fullest spiritual potential.

How to Achieve Your Purpose

1. Have a dream or vision of what he can do for the Lord. I carry in my heart many dreams for my husband's service in the Lord's work. I do not share these dreams with others, but I "ponder them in my heart" as the Bible states that Mary did in Luke 2:19: *"But Mary kept all these things, and pondered them in her heart."* Actually, it is not important that my dreams for him are fulfilled just like I have planned them. I use the dreams not to dictate God's will for his life, but to remember to treat my husband like the special person he can become.

Every husband has bad breath when he wakes up in the morning and smelly feet when he goes to bed at night. Every man has weaknesses and makes mistakes. Still, when we look at our husbands in light of our dreams, we will treat them with more respect.

My husband is a preacher. I wanted to marry a preacher from the time I was a very little girl. I see my husband in light of my dreams for him as a preacher. This causes me to be much more careful about the way I do things for him and about the way I speak to him.

2.   Invest your time in his service for the Lord, especially in the areas of fasting and prayer. When my husband first began traveling and preaching some around the country, I missed him so much that when he arrived home, I was not really interested in what spiritual results had occurred because of his trip. I was mainly interested in having him cheer me up from my loneliness and depression.   Fortunately, I realized that if my attitude continued to be sour, one of two things would happen. Either he would have to quit traveling and doing what I really believed the Lord wanted him to do, or I was going to lose my mind. Not considering either of these to be good alternatives, I decided to do something about what was going on in my mind and heart.

On the first trip my husband took after I made this decision, I made three changes. First, I decided to spend extra time in Bible reading and prayer, especially asking the Lord to give my husband power as he preached. Secondly, I decided to bake something for him as a surprise on his arrival home. I knew that the very act of giving would lift me out of my depression so that I could better share with him the results of his preaching. Thirdly, I decided to fast for Jack's meeting that night. I will never forget the change that took place in my attitude, a change that still carries over into my attitude now. I also will never forget the exciting results that came from that meeting which took place several years ago now. There were sixty-three young people called to full-time Christian service that night. I have met several of them at Hyles-Anderson College where they are preparing for the Lord's work. I met one of them for the first time just a few weeks ago. Each time I meet one of those young people, I can say, "Praise the Lord! I had a part in that." I must admit that I feel completely satisfied.

3. Don't do anything yourself that would hinder him spiritually. I once heard a woman testify who had lost her husband just a few weeks before. He had died suddenly when only in his early forties. The young widow only spoke a few words. They went something like this: "My husband and I were married for twenty years, and we were in full-time Christian work all twenty of those years."

Why were those the words she chose to speak right after her husband's death? I imagine she chose those words because she realized that was all that was really important now that her husband was in Heaven. I doubt if it mattered a whole lot if the garbage was taken out every day or whether the wallpaper ever got hung in the bathroom. What was important to her was that, to the best of her ability, she had not hindered her husband from doing something for God that would last even after his death.

There are a few things in life which I would like to do that I will never do because I feel it would hinder my husband spiritually. There are even some spiritual things I do not do so I can be of more help to him. If I am very successful in some ministry to the extent that my husband is tied down doing things around the house that he would not otherwise have to do, I have failed. If my ministry causes him to see less success in his ministry, I have forgotten my purpose.

For this reason, I believe it is usually a mistake for the wife of a full-time Christian worker to be heavily involved in a career that is outside the ministry. I believe it is best for a woman to be involved in something that will bring her closer to her husband and his ministry. For example, I teach part-time at Hyles-Anderson College where Jack also teaches. Though this is "my baby," so to speak

and my husband has little to do with my class, I am still
able to spend more time with him and to care more about
his ministry because I am doing what I love in a setting that
does not take my heart away from my purpose.

4. See him as more than a provider. I am afraid the
average wife only dreams of her husband getting her a
bigger house, another car, and new clothes. I myself want
to remember that God did not create my spouse to get
material things for me. Though it is the man's responsibility
to provide for his wife, I will definitely be shortchanging
him and his eternal soul if I see him as nothing more than
my provider. My husband was created for a bigger purpose
than that, and so was yours.

5. Don't criticize his service for the Lord. I have
heard women say things such as, "My husband spends so
much time at the church; he should have married the
pastor." The sad thing about such continual nagging is
that those husbands may drop out of church completely.
Then I am sure these same women will be the first ones to
the pastor's office, asking for prayer for their backslidden
husbands.

6. Praise his spiritual victories. A husband will
come nearer to serving the Lord effectively if his wife praises
the good she sees him do. Even if the only good she sees
is his effort, she should praise him rather than criticize him
for his failures.

I'm afraid too many wives, myself included, get more
excited when our husbands get a raise or bring home a new
dress for us than we do when they come home and share
with us that a friend at work just asked Jesus into his heart.
It is no wonder we have more successful businessmen in
the world today than we do men who are turning the world
upside down for Jesus.

7. Last, but certainly not the least, put on the shield of faith. *"Above all, taking the shield of faith, wherewith ye shall be able to quench all the fiery darts of the wicked."* (Ephesians 6:16) Eve did not believe she should not take the fruit because the devil had told her a lie. The devil is telling women the exact same lie today. He is telling us that we cannot depend on God to do what He says He will do. The shield for resisting the devil and the shield for resisting dissatisfaction is faith. The Bible teaches us that our faith grows stronger when we read and hear the preaching of the Word.

Matthew 6:33 says, *"But seek ye first the kingdom of God, and his righteousness; and all these things shall be added unto you."* This verse tells us that if we seek to fulfill our biblical purpose first, God will provide us with the things we need and even with the things we want. What you and I need is the faith to believe this promise. Daily devotions and adherence to the Word as preached from a fiery pulpit is our best assurance of having that faith.

In my own experience, I have been tempted to seek material things first. Each time, the Lord has convicted my heart through His Word and through the preaching I hear at my own church. Up to this point, I think I can say that I have not hindered my husband spiritually. He and I believe that we have been in the center of God's will throughout our married life. The Lord has truly met our needs and many of our wants. Yet, we have been reminded of our purpose and have been privileged to serve the Lord. I must testify that we have been truly satisfied. It is our faith that will continue to preserve us.

Wives, let's not forget our purpose.

CHAPTER II

The Gift of Praise

"As the fining pot for silver, and the furnace for gold; so is a man to his praise." (Proverbs 27:21)

If there is a one-word solution to most marriage problems, I believe that one word would be *praise.* Through praise we can encourage another person to be almost anything we wish that person to be. Proverbs 27:21 says, *"As the fining pot for silver, and the furnace for gold; so is a man to his praise."* Let me illustrate what I believe this verse means.

When I was about eight years old, I wrote a story. After I had finished writing it, I gave a copy to my dad. A few days later, I received a typewritten letter from him in the mail. As a young girl, I was quite impressed because that letter had been typed on my father's church stationery. What the letter said impressed me even more. My dad gave me a gift of praise in that letter that still burns warmly in my heart at the age of thirty-one. He praised me for writing the story. He went on to tell me how proud he was that I not only thought deeply, but that I also wrote down those thoughts on paper. My dad had painted a picture of me that day, and I began to act out the picture that I saw in my mind's eye. To this day, I strive to think deeply and to write down my thoughts on paper. Why? Because when I was eight years old, someone convinced me I was a deep thinker and that what I had to write was important.

Now ask yourself this question: How deep could an eight-year-old girl possibly be? I have asked myself this question often and my answer always seems to be the same: "Not very." I think the deep thinker was my dad. He knew that I was a young and mischievous girl who had an extremely poised and beautiful mother and two sisters as beautiful and talented as she. He knew I might need an identity of my own.

I was perhaps naive enough to believe my father's opinion, which I am sure he expressed sincerely, and to act out my new role as the "deep thinker" of the family. I don't suppose a day goes by that I do not use the gift of praise that I was given so many years ago.

Do you understand how praise can totally affect the outcome of a person's life? Imagine what would have happened if my dad had used my story as fodder for humor around the supper table that night so long ago. I honestly believe the history of my life would have turned out quite differently. Therefore, I believe in giving praise for a very personal reason.

In fact, if I had only one page or if I had less than five minutes in which to share with you how to have a delightful marriage, I would share with you two rules which are both related to that word *praise*. Let me share them with you right now.

- Never say anything negative about your husband.
- Take every opportunity to say something positive about your husband.

Let's discuss rule number one. Never say anything negative about your husband. There is nothing more depressing to my spirit than to hear one person criticize another, especially to hear a person criticize her husband or child or some member of her immediate family. Yet it happens regularly. In fact, it is almost sport for women to get together and criticize their husbands. I have attended bridal showers where I was sure if one more woman made a snide remark about her spouse, the bride would definitely call off the whole thing.

Women need to realize the quality they most admire in a man is how much others respect him. Who determines how much a man is respected? His wife does! Females especially look to a man's wife before they fully develop their opinion of a man. Whether this is right or wrong, it seems typical of female nature. I know that when my pastor-father is preaching and he tells a joke, most of the congregation (especially the women) look to my mother before they decide whether the joke is funny. If she laughs, they laugh.

Many women would never actually say anything critical. They only imply criticism. After all, sometimes things happen for which we do not wish to take the blame. Who better is there to take our blame than that person who is closest to us—our husband? I have heard women say such things as, " I'm sorry I am late, but you know how my husband is." No, I do not know how your husband is, and I do not wish to know.

Let's discuss rule number two. Take every opportunity to say something positive. Actually, there are two approaches to praise. There is the direct approach and the indirect approach. A wife uses the direct approach when she personally gives the gift of praise, whether it be by verbal or written expression. The direct approach of praise is both wonderful and important. Yet it is not always as effective as indirect praise.

For example, sometimes my husband will tell me that I look nice as we are about to leave our house to go somewhere. I hate to admit this, but this praise does not always get through. Sometimes I believe he is only telling me I **look** good because he is trying to **be** nice. You see, a woman usually decides for herself before she leaves the bathroom mirror whether she looks nice. Unfortunately, since she has decided that her hair did not turn out just right and so forth, there is nothing her husband can do to convince her that she really does look attractive.

There have often been times when someone has come to me and shared a compliment that my husband said about me when he was speaking out of town. What happened then is that a dart of praise that he sent out in my absence pierced my mind and reached my heart when he was not present to praise me directly. The fact that my husband thinks enough of me to praise me indirectly impresses me, and I must admit that this type of praise always gets through to my heart.

Now I am not talking about a wife speaking so frequently about her husband to others that folks run when they see her coming. I simply mean that one should plant a little seed of praise here and a little seed there until the praise is scattered everywhere. Yet, if a person is to give praise of her loved ones everywhere she goes, she must genuinely feel it in her heart. Hypocritical praise is both phony and sickening. We must learn to praise sincerely and to praise creatively. Let's begin to see how.

Sincere and Creative Praise

1. Thank the Lord for your husband. Who is more creative than our Saviour? When I begin to thank the Lord

for my husband, the Holy Spirit reminds me of little things that Jack has done for which I have neglected to thank him. Lest anyone think I am insane, the Holy Spirit does not do this audibly. Yet I am sure that I am experiencing real two-way conversation with my God when I pray and thank Him for my husband.

One positive attribute about God is that He is the only Person to Whom you can keep giving and still have more than you had before you gave. That happens with gratitude. The more gratitude I give to God, the more gratitude I have in my heart. The more I thank the Lord for my husband, the more grateful I am for him.

2. Admire him in your mind. My husband and I once talked to a particular couple who was having marital problems. During the conversation, the husband proceeded to tell us every weakness his wife had. He started with her weight, her hairstyle, and her housekeeping, and went on down his list.

Now I don't often speak my mind to someone else's husband and, as a rule, I counsel only women; but I spoke a few words to this husband. What I wanted to say was, "You're not so hot yourself!" I wanted to ask, "Have you looked in the mirror lately?" Thank goodness, I restrained myself. Instead, I shared with this man something that I have had to share with myself often in my marriage. I told him when the day comes that he realizes how lucky he is just to have someone who knows all about him yet accepts him and loves him as he is, he will **begin** to have a workable marriage.

I happen to have someone like that. My husband knows all my weaknesses very well. I guarantee you that they are many. Yet Jack loves me and accepts me as I am. Most people never experience that kind of love and acceptance. Doesn't it seem unreasonable for me then to turn around and require perfection from him? It would be unfair for me to forsake him if he lost his hair or developed a pot belly. It is unfair for weakness to expect perfection.

I know that mid-life crisis can be a real physical problem. However, I believe that a lot of mid-life crisis is just a point a person comes to in his life when he decides that if this is all there is to life, he deserves more. That partially explains why many middle-aged people who have been happily married for many years suddenly forsake their marriage partners.

The truth is that I don't deserve anything. Being loved and accepted by Jack Schaap is just a great big bonus. When I spend some time focusing on his love and his strengths rather than a bald head or a pot belly (he has neither, by the way), I can begin to devise some really sincere and creative praise. Sometimes we need to remind ourselves that we are not so hot and that we are extremely fortunate when we are loved.

My dad has often taught from the pulpit of the First Baptist Church of Hammond, Indiana, that meditation is the key to close relationships. If we are going to give creative praise, we are going to have to meditate. If we are going to meditate, we are probably going to have to set aside time to do so.

3. Admire details. Always saying, "You're great!" can get old and stale. A truly loving wife will take time to notice the details. If she doesn't, no one else will. My husband's boss doesn't have time to go from office to office at Hyles-Anderson College and tell each employee what a fine job he is doing. I surely don't want another woman frequenting Jack's office to tell him what a fine job he is doing. Therefore, if the many different types of effort he

puts in every day get noticed, I am going to have to be the one who notices. If a wife doesn't notice, no one else will. If another female does notice too much, watch out. A man has a tremendous need to be admired and that need influences him.

If you say to me, "I enjoy your writing," that is kind; but it may or may not be convincing. If you say to me, "I enjoyed the idea you expressed on page 95 in the seventh chapter," I am convinced. Why? Because **detailed** praise reaches the heart. What is it about your husband that makes him unique? Notice it and admire him because of it.

4. Praise him in areas where he seems insecure. Every human being has areas in which he feels particularly insecure. Even the most secure men have areas of their lives where they are unsure of themselves. A wise wife will notice these areas and give praise particularly along these lines.

Areas of insecurity will differ according to age, personality, background, and so on. For example, an older man might be insecure about his usefulness. A shy man might be insecure about his ability with people. A small man might be insecure about his strength. If a man has lost his job, he will definitely feel insecure about his ability to support the family. A thoughtful, caring wife will give support and encouragement rather than criticizing the financial condition. This is difficult, yet a man will get back to work quicker if he sees himself as diligent rather than lazy.

Proverbs 20:29 says, *"The glory of young men is their strength: and the beauty of old men is the grey head."* This verse tells us that young men need to feel strong. Since there are not many Charles Atlases walking around, men must often feel insecure about their strength.

This is always a good area in which a wife can give praise.
5. Encourage him to try things. Many women say to
their husbands, "Dear, I think you're wonderful." However,
when he comes home and announces that he is going to try
something new, this same woman is the first to pour cold
water on his idea. Thus, the husband is hearing two
completely different messages. One message says, "I think
you're great." The other says, "I do not have much
confidence in your ideas or abilities."

Why are women so apt to pour cold water on their
husbands' plans? Because we love security and we hate
change. A wife must remember if her husband is going to
succeed, there will be some discomfort and some daring
involved. Both discomfort and daring are things on which
men thrive.

I have tried to learn how to use three words
repeatedly: "Go for it." I do not want my preacher
husband to see his job of reaching and influencing others
in a dull and unimaginative way. Therefore, I must
encourage him to try many avenues of ministry.
Unfortunately, some of his efforts will fail. I must continue
to praise anyway knowing that in this nonchalant world, the
effort is much more important than the success or failure.
The fact that he is happy and visionary in his work is much
more important than his degree of achievement.

You may ask, "What should I do if he comes home
with some really crazy idea that will have permanently
damaging results on our family?" I am not saying that a
wife should never disagree with any of her husband's
opinions. I am saying that her **first** response does not have
to be negative. Your spouse should not think of negativity
as your primary personality trait.

6. Value his ideas and opinions. To express praise

to someone and then totally ignore or ridicule his tastes and opinions is contradictory. A wife should listen to her husband's opinions and try to adjust her appearance, her decorating, or whatever area accordingly.

I do believe that a woman should be the supreme decision maker as far as decorating a home is concerned. A wise husband will let this be his wife's territorial reign. This will give his wife some sense of independence, and it also will prevent many unnecessary squabbles. However, when I go to the store to choose something important for our home, I find more than one sample of something I like. I take these samples home, and Jack chooses the one that he likes best. If he doesn't like any of them, I go to another store and look again. This gives both of us the opportunity of sharing something else together. The more we share, the closer we will be. It also gives me a chance to bring him outside his busy world of the ministry and into my world. Lastly, this shows him that I truly do admire his ideas and opinions.

7. Downplay his weaknesses and defeats. A few years ago, we stopped at a gas station on our way to a speaking engagement. We both got out of the car to buy a snack at the convenience mart. Jack left his keys in the car. I did not realize he had. My thinking at the time was, "What kind of person would leave his car unlocked at a gas station? That is like asking someone to steal it." So, not realizing the keys were still in the ignition and believing you can never be too careful, I locked the car.

I must confess that, once we realized what had happened, we spent the next several minutes arguing about whose fault it was. (If we **had** figured out whose fault it was, it would not have made the keys any less locked in the car.)

Finally, with much embarrassment, we called and asked my husband's assistant to come and pick us up. When we arrived back at the college, I said something to my husband's co-workers like, "I am so absent-minded at times." I assume that they then thought the entire incident was my fault. I know my husband assumed the same thing because he looked at me in complete shock. I actually never did admit blame when I probably should have. Yet I did take the blame for our mishap in front of his co-workers. Why? Because it suddenly mattered more that my husband be respected than that I not seem absent-minded. To be honest, I deeply enjoyed the satisfaction that I got from being such a friend to my husband. That kind of respect makes a marriage a lot richer.

My husband, the partner in this relationship who makes the fewest mistakes by far, covers for me also. Sometimes when I become too tired and irritable at home, he takes our children to another room and keeps them occupied. I often hear him explaining to them that I am tired and that I work hard to take care of the family. What is he doing? He is covering for me lest I lose my children's respect. He could blatantly point out the error of my attitude to them. He could say, "Mom is really in a bad mood. I wonder what her problem is?" Instead, he covers for me when I am weak, and I love him for it.

Remember, a man cannot lead until he has gained the respect of his followers. A wife can do a lot to build that respect by covering for her husband when he is weak. She can also greatly damage his leadership abilities by pointing out and ridiculing his character weaknesses. I love to tease and to be teased, but I try to live by this rule.

Never tease another person
about his character.

8. Never stop praising. It is rare to be around a couple who has been married for several years and still show each other a lot of admiration. This is sad because the more a person cares about someone, the more that person desires the admiration of that someone. Because of this need, admiration and praise become only more important as a relationship matures.

Let me encourage those of you who are up in years to never stop praising your spouse. If you have stopped, maybe you need to start again.

I'm glad someone cared enough when I was a young girl to paint for me a picture of what I could become. I'm glad my dad saw the strength of my story and not the weakness. He gave me a very fine gift that day.

Let's give to others the gift of praise.

CHAPTER III

Accepting Your Husband

*". . . Wherein he hath made us accepted
in the beloved." (Ephesians 1:6)*

A man has two basic needs: admiration and
acceptance. A woman's basic needs are different: love and
security. It is hard for us to understand sometimes, but a
man would rather be admired and accepted for who he is
than to be loved. That is why a man sometimes enjoys the
fellowship of his closest associates at work more than he
enjoys his wife and family. At the work place, he receives
praise and recognition while, sadly, he may receive no
praise at home. This is especially sad because those at
home probably love him more deeply than those at work,
but his family does not recognize the importance of meeting
his most basic needs.

In the previous chapter, I stated that nagging is
making a well-meant suggestion outside one's own realm of
authority. In this chapter, I would like to share eight ways
in which a wife should accept her husband.

No Suggestions Needed

1. Accept the way your husband plans things for
you. Jack and I go on a date every Friday night when we
are in town. I must say that I look forward to those dates
very much. Let's suppose we are going to go on a date

some Friday night and I begin to plan in my mind where I want to go. Teibel's is a good, expensive restaurant located not far from our home. Suppose I decide that I would like to go to Teibel's next Friday night.

Let's imagine that my husband arrives home that night and announces that he would like to go out for pizza and bowling. The discussion might go something like this.

Jack: "I thought we would go out for pizza tonight and then go bowling."

Me: (In a less than enthusiastic voice) "That's fine."

Jack: "What's wrong? Don't you want to go out for pizza and bowling?"

Me: (In a **much** less than enthusiastic voice) "I said that would be fine."

Jack: "Where would you like to go?"

Me: "Well, since you asked . . . I really would like to go to Teibel's."

Jack: "That's fine. Let's go to Teibel's."

Now Jack is a gentleman, and he would gladly take me to Teibel's if that is where I wished to go. However, a man finds tremendous satisfaction in planning things for his wife, and I would have just decreased that desire. I would have also started a habit of always having a better idea than my husband has to offer. The resulting conversation in the future would go something like this.

Jack: "Where would you like to go tonight?"

Me: "I don't know. Where would you like to go?"

Jack: "I don't know. Where would you like to go?"

Me: "Don't you have any plans? You never plan things for me anymore."

Because a wife has a tremendous need to have

things planned for her, I would become disenchanted with my husband. I am not saying that a wife is rebellious if she plans her evenings with her husband. I **am** saying that she is pretty stupid. I want the pleasure of having him plan things for me. If I want to have that pleasure, I must sacrifice a few things. I may have to go for pizza when I wanted to go to Teibel's, and I may have to go to Teibel's when I wanted to go bowling. Not getting my way is a small price to pay for having a man who plans things for me.

There is nothing wrong with sharing your wish to go somewhere with your husband at another more appropriate time. However, when the plans have already been made, I would recommend that you follow his plans. This is one of those small areas where you can assure him that he is indeed the leader of your relationship.

2. Accept his gifts. A man puts a tremendous amount of his personality and ego in the choosing of a gift for his wife. To reject that gift is to reject him. You should not be selfish when receiving a gift from your husband. Rather, have fun seeing how good you can make him feel about the gift that he has given.

Sometimes a man may give a gift that seems practical and unromantic. You must remember that a man is a need-filler. When he gives a practical gift (such as the much talked about frying pan), it is not because he has lost his romantic attraction for you. It is probably because he saw a need and decided to fill it. A woman should never reject a practical gift from her husband. She can, however, be careful about what type of needs she expresses (especially right before Christmas). While they are shopping, a wife might also give her husband ideas about the kind of things she **would** like to receive from him. Still, the time that the gift is being given should be a time of total acceptance.

3. Accept the way he works. Jack is a full-time administrator and faculty member at Hyles-Anderson College. Though we are "one flesh," I was not called to do his job with him. I did not interview for the job, nor was I asked by his boss, Dr. Wendell Evans, to do his job. Therefore, I should not make suggestions about his job performance.

We work very differently. I am a fast worker. I do a considerable amount of work in a day's time. Yet, at times, I leave some very loose ends to the jobs I have done. On the other hand, Jack is a perfectionist who will complete a job down to the last detail in a first-class manner. Because I am in his office two days a week, I could be tempted to make suggestions about his work. Still, this is not my realm of authority. I do not know best how to do his job. Even if I did know best, I would rather he fail at his job than to give him my nagging suggestions. If he fails, he can get back up as a grown man and go on.

As a preacher's wife, let me stress how important it is not to make suggestions about your husband's preaching. When you make suggestions to him about his full-time Christian work, you may be hindering the work of the Holy Spirit. The Holy Spirit does not reveal to you what your husband should preach; He reveals it to him. We do not always understand the workings of the Holy Spirit in the life of one of His servants. I certainly do not want to hinder the workings of the Holy Spirit in my husband's life.

4. Accept the way he schedules his time. I am a duty person. I love to make lists of things to do and to see those items checked off my list as I complete them. The liability of this is that I struggle to really be there for people when they need me.

Jack is a people person. He makes his lists and has a great sense of duty, but he would drop almost anything to help another person. Because of this flexibility, we schedule our time very differently. It would be tragic for me to try to change him into being like me or vice versa.

It would be wonderful if everyone were perfectly balanced in their attitudes toward people and duties. Yet if we reach that goal in every area of our lives, it will take a lifetime. As we are trying to achieve this goal, we should accept the other person and his differences. If we believe that God creates every person for his individual purpose, then we will also realize that God is going to instill in each individual his own unique character traits. The traits of one man can seem like weaknesses to another man when, in reality, those traits may be necessary equipment for the task God has for that one man to do.

How tragic that wives spend so much time trying to remake their husbands rather than trying to encourage them by prayer, praise, and action.

5. Accept the way he handles people. I have found that most of the ministry involves dealing with people. My husband and I often tease that we would love the ministry if only there were no people involved. Where there are people and relationships, there are problems with which to contend. There are times when I may think my husband is too hard on a person. There may be times when I think he is too easy. There are times when he says something to someone, and I wish that he had not. I'm sure there are times when he wishes I had given more time and compassion to a particular person. Nevertheless, I believe that it is outside my realm of authority to make suggestions to my spouse about the way he handles people.

Now there may be times when you need to discuss

with your husband some impropriety that may be taking place, especially when it comes to a member of the opposite sex. Still, I would not discuss such matters without much prayer so I can be sure such a discussion should take place. If you are constantly making suggestions about your husband's handling of people, you are probably becoming a nag.

Oftentimes, a very outgoing man who talks first and thinks later will marry a very shy and soft-spoken young lady. Perhaps a reserved young man will marry an extremely outspoken woman. These couples will be headed for divorce unless they learn to accept the way their spouses handle people. An important thing to realize is that **we are not always right.** We may be very convinced that our opinions are right, yet our opinion can still be wrong. For example, I may think my husband treated someone too harshly, and I may have a pretty good track record when it comes to dealing with people. However, the possibility still exists that I **could be** wrong; furthermore, when it comes to deciding what someone else should do regarding handling people, there is a very good chance that **I am** wrong.

Sometimes a wife nags her husband because he is not close to her family or to someone to whom she wishes he would be close. Let me just state here that the worst way to improve a relationship between a family member or a friend and your husband is to begin to make suggestions about his behavior around that person.

6. Accept his affection. When your husband reaches out to express affection to you and you reject it, he feels rejected. You may **say,** "Not right now, dear; I'm doing the dishes." But he **hears,** "I reject you."

A key word in the marriage relationship is *respond.*

Respond to your husband's every word and action with an **appropriate response.** When he arrives home, respond. When he leaves, respond. When he tells a story or a joke, respond. When he gives you a hug, respond with an appropriate response. An appropriate response would not be to stand there like a dead fish. Throw your arms around him in warm reciprocation.

7. Accept his preferences. My husband has some preferences. One of his preferences is that the mirror that comes out from the wall in his bathroom be left without the magnifying side facing the front. This may sound silly to some, yet I try to remember to put the mirror on the right side and satisfy his preferences. I'm afraid that most marital arguments are about little things like preferences. I would like to be the kind of wife who looks for ways to satisfy preferences, not the kind who reacts negatively to every preference my husband expresses.

8. Accept his toys. Every well-balanced man has a hobby. Someone has said that a woman has hobbies, too; hers are just less expensive! It is easy for a wife to see her hobby as sensible and profitable while she views her husband's hobby as a threat to her and a waste of time.

When a young girl gets married, she begins to make her husband her whole world. While a young man does not love his new bride any less than she loves him, he is more prone to make her just a part of his life. That is why he can get home from his honeymoon one day and call from work the next day to announce to his bride that he wants to play basketball with his friends. This can be devastating to a young bride. She is apt to think, "How could he love me and want to spend time with anyone other than me?"

If this bride is not careful, she will consider basketball to be the enemy. Whenever one spouse hates

something that the other loves, a wall begins to be
constructed. Don't allow basketball (or anything else) to
become a wall; make it a bridge. You build your bridge by
saying, "Go ahead and play basketball with your friends. I
want you to have a good time, and I want you to promise
me that you will take me somewhere to shoot some baskets
with you sometime." Then check out books on basketball
at the library, order a subscription to a sports magazine, or
watch basketball on television—do what you can to learn to
know and love basketball. Your husband will then learn to
associate having a good time not so much with his friends,
but with you. Hopefully, you will become his best friend.

My husband loves to hunt. While the men in my
family have been very athletic, they are not hunters. When
my father sees a deer scampering across a meadow, he
thinks of the beauty of God's nature. When my husband
sees the same deer, he wishes he had his rifle with him.
Because of my family's lack of familiarity with hunting, I
could have hated it. However, Jack and I have fond
memories of autumn walks in the woods looking for good
spots for hunting. We have some pretty humorous
memories of early morning duck hunts together. I have not
hunted with him often because I cannot sit still for very
long and tend to be somewhat noisy. (My husband and I
are opposite in that respect, too.) Still, I can honestly say
that I love hunting. As autumn approaches, my thoughts
turn to the excitement of hunting season. Jack rarely has
the time to hunt. He has to spend his leisure on less
time-consuming hobbies as he grabs a moment here and
there. Still, at one time in our lives, hunting was a bridge
that has provided us with some wonderful memories.

One evening while waiting for him to get cleaned up
after work for one of our dates, I began to read the only

magazine in the room which happened to be a hunting magazine. When he entered the room, he asked what I was reading. I said I was reading a hunting magazine. He responded by saying very affectionately, "I like you!" I'm glad I learned to like hunting.

God can even instill certain hobbies into a person's life to prepare that person for working with certain types of people. A man without any interests other than his work or ministry may become a workaholic. Let's accept our husbands' pleasures as well as we accept their work.

Before closing this chapter, let me share some things that a wife should not do if she is going to accept her husband as he is.

Advice Seldom Heeded

1. Don't correct him. The following are some areas in which a wife should avoid correcting her husband.

- Don't correct him when he tells a story. We may make ourselves look smart, but we make him look ignorant.
- Don't correct him when he tells a joke.
- Don't correct his English.
- Don't correct his job performance. A preacher's wife should not motion to her husband from the pew to correct a mistake he has made in the pulpit.
- Don't correct his appearance. I am careful not to straighten my husband's tie, remove lint from his jacket, etc. in public. Sometimes, the disrespect we show our husbands can be more embarrassing than the actual flaw in their appearance.

Sometimes a wife corrects her husband to be sure he gives the right impression. I would correct something that would be a huge source of embarrassment to my husband.

Yet, as a rule, I take the attitude that he is going to give a great impression without my help. I am going to give him my confidence and not my correction.

2. Don't laugh at him. There is a big difference in laughing **with** and laughing **at** a person. Sometimes our roaring laughter, especially about jokes in which husbands are the punch line, can be a manifestation of disrespect. Remember, we determine to a great degree whether our husband is respected. Therefore, be careful not to show disrespect in any area.

3. Don't accept your husband based on what he does. While a wife is to be bringing out her husband's fullest spiritual potential, she should not become the judge of his job performance. A husband will stand before the Lord for himself and for his individual responsibilities. Our responsibility is to encourage him. We will stand before the Lord and give account of how well we fulfilled our purpose. We will not give account for our husbands.

4. Don't think about his weaknesses. If any woman decides to spend a whole day thinking about her husband's weaknesses, she can be ready for the divorce court by the end of the day. On the other hand, if she concentrates on his strengths for an entire day, she will realize how fortunate she is to be his wife.

5. Don't compare your husband with other men. There is often a tendency for a young wife to compare her husband with older and more successful men. This is a terrible mistake. I'm glad my husband was not as mature as some older men whom I admired when we got married. If he had been, I know a nineteen-year-old bride who would have lagged far behind. It has been a joy to grow and mature together.

In closing, let me remind you that God is preparing

your husband for his individual task. Only God is fully aware of the necessary ingredients needed to complete the recipe. Please don't tamper with His recipe. Rather, treat him with tender loving care. Make full use of the opportunity to complete your husband through prayer, praise, and action. Other than that, our job is easy.

Let's just accept our husbands for exactly who they are.

CHAPTER IV

The Root of the Problem

"And he said unto me, My grace is sufficient for thee: for my strength is made perfect in weakness. Most gladly therefore will I rather glory in my infirmities, that the power of Christ may rest upon me." (II Corinthians 12:9)

As I have stated earlier, there is just about a 50-percent divorce rate in the United States today. I would like to devote this chapter to what I believe is the root of that problem—biblical self-acceptance. I hope you will notice that I said **biblical** self-acceptance.

Everyone seems to be grasping for self-acceptance. Even secular psychiatrists seem to comprehend that lack of self-acceptance causes bad marriages as well as ruined lives. Yet the self-acceptance these psychiatrists teach is very different from that learned through God's Word.

I'm not talking about a type of self-acceptance that causes us to spend hours in front of the mirror repeatedly saying things such as, "I'm great." Though I believe that self-acceptance is an important concept with teachings that can be found in the Bible, I also believe that the methods for finding it are very different from those taught in the world today. Furthermore, I believe many churches are teaching a type of self-acceptance that is not biblical. I would rather call it self-indulgence or self-pride.

What, then, is biblical self-acceptance? Let me illustrate.

When I was a child, I was almost deathly afraid of storms. Every time the sky became just a little bit threatening, I panicked. When I would go to my mom and dad with my fears, they would tell me to "trust God." As a child, those words seemed so trite and unpractical for earthly living. You see, I felt if God could be trusted, there would not have been dark clouds in the sky in the first place.

When I became a teenager, most of my fear of storms vanished. Other fears came to replace that fear. I still was admonished by adults, not only at home but also at the church and the Christian school where I attended, to "trust God." Yet I still could not comprehend what it meant to trust God, nor did I understand how to measure my trust.

I do not especially like to admit this, but when I was about sixteen years old, the worst thing I could imagine happening to me would be for God to call me to Africa to be a missionary. I can honestly say that thought has seemed appealing to me as an adult at times, but when I was a teenager, I thought it was the worst thing that could happen. In my yet very immature mind, I asked myself if I would trust God if He called me to be a missionary to Africa. When the answer came back, "I don't think so," I incorrectly decided that I must not trust God very much.

As a teenager, there was one other thing I thought would be the worst thing that could happen to a person (and I must admit that my feelings about this have not changed very much). I felt then, and still do, that one of the worst things that could happen would be to have a child of my own become very sick with a disease, such as leukemia. I did not feel I could bear seeing a small child suffer when he was not old enough to understand his pain.

So I asked myself, "Would I trust God if He gave me a child someday and that child had leukemia?" The answer came back, "I don't think so." After answering these questions, I decided I must not trust God very much, and even sadder was the fact that I did not see how I ever could.

I'm not so sure that my problem back then was really a lack of trust. Rather, I believe it was a misunderstanding of what it meant to trust God. I did not realize until I was an adult that trust is not measured by what you might do if God sent a problem in your life in the future. It is measured by what you are doing about the problems He sends in your life today. **Trust is accepting everything God has placed in your life until this moment.**

Many married adults (or unmarried for that matter) have readily accepted all the many gifts God has given them: a healthy body, food to eat, and air to breathe. Often, they have accepted those gifts without acknowledging the One Who provided them. Yet very many, if not most people, have done very little accepting of the negative things that have happened in their lives. If someone has hurt them, they have held grudges. If their parents annoyed them, they have rebelled against them. If their brothers or sisters irritated them, they have ignored them or sought revenge against them. I'm afraid this is the state the average person is in when he comes to the marriage altar.

Yet, romance is a very attractive thing. Many a young person has headed toward a marriage altar just sure she can accept the person to whom she is about to say "I do" even though she has not accepted anything or anyone who has gone against her will so far. Herein lies perhaps the most basic cause for our high divorce rate in this country. A bitter young man marries a bitter young lady, and that bitterness is soon lashed out upon each other. The cycle of bitterness starts all over.

II Corinthians 12:9 says, *". . . My grace is sufficient for thee . . ."* I believe this phrase can be our best cure for bitterness and unhealthy marriages and our best antidote for lack of self-acceptance. Let me explain what I think this verse can teach us by sharing with you the following four points.

The Underlying Answer

1. We all have deficiencies. Nobody is perfect. All of us have something about which we could be bitter. Perhaps you are too fat or too skinny. Perhaps your hair is too thick or too thin. Maybe your deficiency goes a little deeper and you are the victim of divorce or child abuse. Maybe you did not know your father; or worse yet, you knew him, loved him, and watched him walk away, never to return. Maybe you have dealt with handicaps or illnesses in your life. All of us have known what it is like to be deeply hurt by a friend.

None of us are perfectly complete people. We all are like puzzles with pieces missing. Yet God commands us in Matthew 5:48, *"Be ye therefore perfect, even as your Father which is in heaven is perfect."* The Bible word *perfect* does not mean to be without sin. Rather, it means to be complete. How can we be complete if we all have deficiencies—things that have caused our lives to this point to be imperfect? The next point gives us the answer.

2. God has the exact (or sufficient) amount of grace needed to complete us. God has the exact puzzle pieces we are missing to make us complete as His children. At Hyles-Anderson College, I have known bus kids so poised and

seemingly so well-trained that I was shocked when I learned they had not grown up in secure Christian homes. Those young people were living proof of the completing grace of God. God can make us as complete as those who have not had our disadvantages.

3. If we reject our deficiencies, God will not give us His grace. If we are bothered by our imperfect appearance and discontent with our financial condition or our personality quirks, God will not send His grace to our bitter hearts. Perhaps we cannot forgive a mom or dad with whom we did not get along. If not, God will not be able to complete us with His grace.

4. If we accept our deficiencies, God fills us with grace so that our deficiencies are unnoticeable to others. Raneé Bullard is a friend who used to live only a few blocks from where I live. She is now a pastor's wife in Groves, Texas. At one time, her husband was an assistant pastor at the First Baptist Church of Hammond. It was during this time that I got to know her better.

Raneé had polio as a child, and the disease left her slightly crippled. Whenever I was with Raneé, I could not remember that she had any handicap. I'm afraid this caused me to be inconsiderate of her at times. I just forgot she was handicapped.

Why did I forget? Mainly because Raneé radiated a personality and charm that came from having accepted her handicap a long time ago. Raneé called her handicap God's special mark upon her life. When she submitted her life to the Lord and accepted her handicap, the Lord made Raneé's handicap invisible to folks like myself. Who says God doesn't work miracles in this age!

God has certainly worked a miracle in my life. You see, I am the youngest and was the most mischievous of the

Hyles children. Yet as I have grown in my relationship with
the Lord and have learned to accept myself as I am—clumsy,
mischievous, and all—I have seen that the Lord can use me
in such a way that my weaknesses are much less noticeable,
even to myself. There is a song that goes something like
this: "It's a miracle that God could make a miracle of me."
I often sing that song around the house, and I am grateful
for the miracle He performs by way of His grace.

　　　Therefore, if we truly trust God, it is not because we
would go to Africa if He called us. None of us will know
whether we would go until He calls. Nor will any of us
know what our response would be if our child were deathly
ill. We do know what our response was when we stubbed
our toe yesterday. We know how we acted when our
husband came home late from work or when our child
spilled Koolaid on the carpet. We know how we are
responding to the incidents in our past and present that
have left us disappointed by people or circumstances. Our
responses to the problems that God has already placed in
our lives is a better way to measure our trust.

　　　It is our bitterness that shows our lack of trust and
hinders God's work in our lives and in our relationships.
In fact, I tell the girls in my Christian Wife class at Hyles-
Anderson College, "If you are bitter about **anything**, you
are not ready to get married."

　　　Allow me to share seven things that the Christian
wife may have a hard time accepting.

Unchangeables

　　　1. Her Appearance. Each semester I teach self-
acceptance in my college class. I often ask my students to
write down some things they have a hard time accepting in
their lives. Their answers usually vary greatly. Yet it seems

that each girl has one answer similar to every other's. It has something to do with her appearance.

I came to the point in my life when I decided if so few people were satisfied with their appearance, I might as well learn to accept mine. When I was a teenager, I remember seeing an advertisement in a magazine for a particular shade of lipstick. The model in the advertisement was a beautiful girl with long, blonde hair. Because I admired the way she looked in the ad, I ran out to the drugstore and bought the same lipstick. When I came home, I discovered something very interesting. Though I had bought the same shade of lipstick, I still did not look a thing like the model in the advertisement. That should have been obvious to me because I am a brunette. Yet there was something in my subconscious mind that made me long to look different.

There are many things we can do to alter our appearance. We can buy a new lipstick or a new dress. We can try a new hairstyle or a new diet. I do believe in doing our best with ourselves. Yet God has given us a basic facial appearance, skin type, etc. which will linger with us for as long as we live. I must admit that I have grown tired of looking at the same person in the mirror for thirty-one years. Yet most of my appearance is never going to change, so why should I make myself miserable by rejecting the looks God has planned for me?

This may sound like an unimportant topic to be discussing in a marriage manual. However, I think I am accurate when I say that the majority of girls who get married have not really accepted the way they look. Perhaps they feel pretty on their wedding day, but there is something about their looks that they are waiting to change. Often, these are unalterable characteristics.

I believe that accepting one's appearance is just the beginning phase of self-acceptance. Until we have reached it, we cannot go on to something else. I'm afraid that many married ladies have not reached square one. If you can change your appearance and you feel that the Lord would have you to do so, then change it. If you cannot, accept how you look as a gift from the Father's hand.

2. Her Personality. Most of us have things we do not like about our personalities. While some of us are too introverted, others of us are too extroverted. While some of us are too shy and quiet, others of us are too loud. While some of us are workaholics, others of us fight laziness. While some of us are hot-tempered, others of us are unable to share our feelings with others. I could go on and on.

Balance and a Christ-like personality should be our goals. These are goals which I am hopefully growing closer to achieving. I have moved away from the introverted person that I was. I have moved away from the sometimes inappropriately loud and stubborn person that I was. Yet even at the age of thirty-one, I often disappoint myself and revert to the old nature that I thought I had left behind. I'm sure you do the same at times.

Our response to ourselves and others when we do this is a good revealer of our ability to accept our personalities. You see, God made my personality as it is with both strengths and weaknesses. God does not expect me to glory in my weaknesses; neither does He expect me to berate myself when I fail or when I do not measure up to someone else. What I see as a weakness in my life may well be a characteristic God has given to equip me for His will for my life.

I must accept my personality as God planned it. I

will grow out of my weaknesses if I depend on the Lord. Yet the framework of whom Cindy Schaap is will remain the same. Because of this framework, the old me will resurface time and time again. Still, God can use even my failures to enable me to better help others.

I have known many wonderful ladies through the ministries of First Baptist Church of Hammond. Some are loud and some are quiet. Some are actively involved in a full-time ministry and others are busy at home with a house full of children. Each lady can afford to learn from the others, however none of them can afford to reject her personality as God made it.

3. Her Parents. One of the most important things a girl needs to accept are the people of her past. If she has not accepted the people of her past, particularly her own family, she has not accepted herself and is therefore poorly equipped to accept anyone in her future.

A girl especially needs to accept her father. A father is a girl's first love. Through her father, a girl not only learns about God, but she also learns how to love her future husband. Our daughter Jaclynn has a sweet, special love relationship with her daddy. She told him a few years ago that she wanted to marry him. She also said that if she could not marry him, she would like her husband to build a house in our back yard so she could always be near him.

I am grateful for their relationship, and my prayer is that it will always be one where the two can accept each other. Why? Because the father-daughter relationship and the husband-wife relationship are entwined. In fact, all our relationships are related to one another.

To understand this better, think back to the last time you had an argument with your husband. You may remember that you did not get along with the other employees at work that day either. Perhaps you will recall that you were curt with your friend on the phone and just did not feel like talking. You may have yelled at your children or complained that the preacher's sermon was too long that day. Then perhaps you climbed in bed at the end of the day and wondered what was wrong with everybody.

The fact is, there was nothing wrong with "everybody." There was something wrong with your attitude about one of your relationships. You see, whenever we feel bitterness toward another person, it is not because of that person and the circumstances he may have caused. It is because we are bitter in our hearts. We cannot control others, but we can control our hearts.

When a girl has a bitter heart toward her father, that heart also will show bitterness in her marriage relationship. Because a father teaches his daughter about love, that daughter's marriage relationship will be similar to the relationship she had with her father unless she deals with any bitterness that still exists.

I was extremely close to my dad when I was growing up. I spent much time with him and learned to trust his love. I also grew to be very thoughtful of him and found great satisfaction in that. Obviously, there are differences in my marriage relationship, but there are also great similarities. I feel I am extremely close to my husband and well-equipped to share the heartbeat of his ministry because I shared my dad's ministry with him for so many years. I hate to think what my marriage would have been like had I been bitter against or thoughtless of my dad for all those years.

On the other hand, a young man learns to love from his relationship with his mother; therefore, his attitude toward his mom is very important. Notice I said that his attitude is important. A young man whose mother abandoned or mistreated him may not have been provided with a very good start in learning how to love. However, he can still have a good marriage if he does not hold bitterness toward his mother. His attitude is the key.

4. Her Past. Almost every person's past carries some negative experiences, but one who rejects her past is really rejecting herself. Romans 8:28 says, *"And we know that all things work together for good to them that love God, to them who are the called according to his purpose."* God works for good all things that happen in our lives. He can take the disadvantage of growing up in a non-Christian home and make it work for our good. He can take child abuse, divorce, or even our own sin and make it good. It is never good that we have sinned, yet God's grace makes us usable. God enables us to help others who have sinned after we have confessed and repented of that same sin.

If we are angry and bitter about anything that has happened in our past, we cannot have a marriage based on self-acceptance. God will not complete us with His grace and work good in that area of our lives. The key is in our acceptance of His grace. He promises to take every bad circumstance in our lives and turn it into good. Sounds like a miracle to me! What an amazing God we have!

All of us have people in our past who have hurt us or disappointed us. Some of these are family members. God knew what He was doing when He put those people in our families. If we really trust God, we will accept every person and circumstance which He has placed in our past up until this very moment.

5. Her Present. Some of us have accepted the hurts and disadvantages of our past, but we are not dealing very well with the present. Perhaps we resent our financial

condition. I have known people with limited financial resources who went from person to person saying, "Pray for me. I'm in bad shape financially." When one says this, he magnifies his weakness and causes us to think of him as poor. I have known others who had equally limited financial resources, but you would never have known it by their attitude. Therefore, I did not see them as poor. If we do not magnify the weaknesses of our present condition, anyone else who is worth his salt will not either.

Have you ever noticed how unappealing a miserable pregnant lady looks? On the other hand, have you ever noticed how cute a happy pregnant lady looks? That is a pretty good illustration of how our attitude determines how people view our condition.

Perhaps you are having a hard time accepting where you live. Yet we must realize that even the house or apartment where we live is a reflection of ourselves. When we do not accept the present environment where God has placed us, we are really rejecting ourselves. It is good to do our best with our environment. Yet we also must remember that any person with a proper perspective realizes that the size or price tag of one's house is not important. Rather, what makes one person more desirable than another is the radiance of his or her spirit or attitude. We cannot radiate the spirit of Christ until we are accepting ourselves and our present circumstances.

6. Her Future. Often when a person refuses to do God's will in his life, he excuses it by saying, "I just want to be myself."

My dad and pastor, Dr. Jack Hyles, preached a sermon several years ago that I believe was entitled "The Real You Is in There Somewhere." In that sermon, he explained that the real you is that person whom God made you to be. Therefore, when you reject God's calling, you are really rejecting yourself.

Many people reject their future because they feel unqualified to do the task to which God might be calling them. If there is anything I have learned about the Christian life, it is that I cannot do anything unless I depend completely upon God. I have also learned that I can do great things while depending upon God, and so can you.

Others reject their future because they fear God will call them to do something they do not wish to do. God is good not only to call us to a particular task, but also to give us the desire and grace with which to do it. As a teenager, it was needless for me to worry about going to Africa or having a sick child. If God calls me to endure something in my future, He also will give me the grace to bear it.

I have found that much of what I have been called to do for God has coincided very closely with the desires I have had since childhood. He has not planned it exactly as I would have; He has planned it much better.

7. Her Talent. Many people do not accept their future as planned by God because they do not realize they have valuable talents given to them by God for His service. People who do not recognize and use their talents for the Lord are not fully accepting themselves. These people are like the unwise servant in the Bible who buried his talent. *"Then he which had received the one talent came and said, Lord, I knew thee that thou art an hard man, reaping where thou hast not sown, and gathering where thou has not strawed: And I was afraid, and went and hid thy talent in the earth: lo, there thou hast that is thine."* (Matthew 25:24-25)

Too often we think of talent as limited to only a few things, like playing the piano, singing, etc. There are many

other talents which are equally important. Let me list a few:
- The ability to relate well with children
- The ability to make people feel better about themselves after you have been with them
- The ability to smile beautifully
- The ability to be extremely helpful and thoughtful
- The ability to discuss and express love well in marriage
- The ability to endure pain
- The ability to persevere

If I could choose the most important talents, I would choose some of those mentioned above. I did not even mention the more obvious talents, such as artistic abilities, leadership abilities, writing abilities, etc. **All of us have talent and it is a sin for us to reject those talents and refuse to use them for the Lord.**

Some of us do not use our talents because we are too busy trying to develop unnatural talents. For example, I believe that it is usually unwise (not always) for a middle-aged woman to try to learn to play the piano for the first time, **especially if she is doing it to improve her self-esteem.** It generally does not help one's self-esteem to play "Mary Had a Little Lamb" on the piano at age forty. It would be better for that same lady to use the talents God has already given her to glorify the Lord.

Yes, I agree that it is never too late to learn something new. Yet God's will for our lives is better determined by checking the path on which He has led us heretofore, examining the gifts we have developed along the way, and using every one in whatever way we can for the Lord. In using our God-given gifts, we often develop more talents while using those we already have.

In closing, let me say it was a very good day in my

life when I learned to accept the big and especially the little things that God places in my life *each day*. Whatever comes my way, be it good or bad, I am learning to take a deep breath and receive my circumstances as from the Father's hand, because that is exactly where they come from. In doing this, I have learned to accept every little detail about Cindy Schaap. God certainly has taken a lot of positive and negative and worked it out to be very good. Truly His grace is sufficient as long as I will accept it.

Let us accept His grace so that we can accept ourselves, and then begin accepting our closest neighbor— our husband.

CHAPTER V

Proper Priorities

"But seek ye first the kingdom of God, and his righteousness: and all these things shall be added unto you." (Matthew 6:33)

Have you ever known a lady who seemed to have done everything in her life and to have done it well? I have. In fact, that type of lady seems to exist in abundance in our church. Have you ever compared yourself with those ladies and felt frustrated at your lack of accomplishment? I must admit that I have, and I'm sure that others have also. One day, however, it dawned on me that those ladies whom I admire and I have one thing in common. Each of us can basically do only one thing at any given time. True, we may be able to stir the soup and talk on the phone simultaneously but, as a rule, we produce our best when we give our minds and efforts to one thing at a time. (If you are absent-minded like I am, doing only one thing at a time prevents disaster and saves lives.) Because every lady can only do one thing at a time, she has some choices to make. At any given moment, she has to decide what is most worthy of her time right then. This is why priorities are important. When we know our priorities, we are less tempted to compare ourselves with others because we know what God expects of us.

There is another observation I would like to make before I share my priority list with you, but I would like to share this example first.

A few years ago, a student in my Christian Wife class came to me seeking some advice. She was engaged to be married and was just weeks away from graduating from college. Her fiancé, however, had another year of college. They were engaged to be married after his graduation.

This young lady had been offered a job working in a Christian home for wayward children. The opportunity excited her because it was along the line of her general interests. Her plan was to work at the children's home in a distant state during the year of her engagement while her fiancé was several hundreds of miles away finishing his college education. This dedicated Christian asked my advice about her tentative plans.

Before I give you my answer, imagine with me what might have happened. Let's suppose this girl, whom I will call Ann, decided to take the job in the children's home. Imagine that she had worked in that children's home for a year then decided she had made a mistake by spending that year away from her fiancé. Would it be possible for Ann to go to her fiancé and ask him if she could relive their engagement year over or if they could postpone their wedding for another year? After all, engagement is a very special time and usually happens only once. In spite of this, I don't think this fiancé, whom I will call Ed, would be very pleased about postponing his wedding another year. There is very little possibility that Ann will have another opportunity to enjoy her engagement as she would like to have.

Now let's suppose Ann decided to stay close to Ed during their engagement and turned down the opportunity to work in the children's home. Is there a possibility she will have another chance to work with children in Christian service during her lifetime? The answer is probably "Yes."

Based on this example, allow me to make this observation. I have found in my life that opportunities come, go, and usually come back again, but stages of relationships do not. This is a good observation to remember when a wife is establishing her priorities.

Successful leaders will often admonish people to "seize the opportunity" because it may never return. This is often good advice, especially for people who tend to be shy, reticent, or maybe just plain lazy when it comes to getting involved in the Lord's work. However, the devil can use this kind of advice to ruin a person like myself who becomes intrigued by almost every opportunity that comes her way.

A Two-Word Priority List

A Christian woman must remember that she was not created primarily to seize her own opportunities; she was created to be a helpmeet to a man. Therein lies the big difference between the priorities of a man and a woman. A man is called to a work, and a woman is called to a man. Therefore, I have established a little two-word priority list for the Christian wife.

1. People
2. Duties

The priority list for a man would be very different. A woman is called to serve people. When I say a woman should put people before duties, I am not saying she should not do her housekeeping so she can talk for hours on the phone to her best friend. Nor do I mean that her social life should come before her church work. Rather, I am saying that a woman should put **the people with whom God has entrusted her** before her duties.

God has entrusted me at this time with a husband and two children. Their care is my responsibility. Someday I may have elderly parents or someone else who depends upon me for their primary care. At this time, however, I have three people whom God has entrusted to me, so they take priority over my duties. In every area of the Christian life, balance is the key. *"A false balance is abomination to the Lord: but a just weight is his delight."* (Proverbs 11:1) It would not be good for my family or for me if I catered to their every whim and did not allow myself to have any life apart from them. However, I must be sure their physical needs as well as their spiritual and emotional needs take priority over my duties.

Before a new bride or a new mother decides to launch herself into a full-time career, she should ask herself if she will still have time to savor her relationships and to be what she needs to be to the people with whom God has entrusted her. Young marriages and young children change and grow up. I have found in my life, however, that opportunities are usually still around when the different stages of my relationships have passed.

In establishing my priority list, I first asked myself this question, "Why was I made as a human being?" The answer I find in the Scriptures is to fellowship with God. Mark 12:30 says, *"And thou shalt love the Lord thy God with all thy heart, and with all thy soul, and with all thy mind, and with all thy strength: this is the first commandment."*

1. Fellowship with God is my first priority. Though I believe that following the other commandments in the Bible is very important, I'm afraid there are some Christians

who see Christianity as revolving around a lifestyle rather than around a Person, Jesus Christ. The secret to being a good Christian is knowing and loving the Person. When we love Him, our obedience should follow.

I believe that is why we sometimes hear of Christians who did so much good in the Lord's service but eventually dropped out and cannot be found serving the Lord at all. When we become motivated by anything that replaces our love for Jesus Christ, we will eventually "burn out" and quit the race. James 1:12 says, *"Blessed is the man that endureth temptation: for when he is tried, he shall receive the crown of life, which the Lord hath promised to them that love him."* I believe this verse teaches not only that we will receive a crown if we endure temptation, but that only those who are motivated by love for Jesus will be **able** to endure. If we are going to love Jesus enough to endure until the race is finished, we must know Jesus very well.

While I know that Jesus is everywhere and I can speak to Him whenever I wish, I still believe that every Christian wife needs a set time and place when she does nothing but seek the Lord. I find I need about an hour a day, at least, to be the kind of Christian I should be. I have a feeling if I need that, others need it also.

As a child, I was taught that there are four things we should do with the Bible:

- Read it.
- Study it.
- Memorize it.
- Meditate upon it.

Because of this teaching, I read several chapters a day from different locations in the Bible so I can have several different types of needs filled. I also have a set time each week when I study the Bible. Daily, I memorize two new verses from the Bible while reviewing two old verses. I keep track of the verses I have memorized by writing the references in the back of my Bible. I tried using index cards, but lost them once and decided to use the back of my Bible instead. I must confess that I read my Bible for many years before I began memorizing it like I should. After I had been memorizing the Bible for several years, a sweet young Christian wife in our church named Joanne Bass encouraged me to memorize complete chapters and books of the Bible. This recommendation has helped me tremendously. Nothing has strengthened my faith and given me wisdom through these last couple of years like Bible memorization has. When you memorize the Bible, it is not hard to meditate upon it throughout the day. *"This book of the law shall not depart out of thy mouth; but thou shalt meditate therein day and night, that thou mayest observe to do according to all that is written therein: for then thou shalt make thy way prosperous, and then thou shalt have good success."* (Joshua 1:8)

I prefer praying and reading my Bible out loud. While I have prayed many a prayer on a lawn tractor or on a bicycle, I prefer the kneeling position. To my knowledge, this is the only praying position referred to in the Bible. I am not a great Christian, but all that I am I owe to the sweet fellowship I have with Christ.

In establishing my second priority, I asked myself, "Why was I made as a woman?" To be a helpmeet to my husband. *"And the Lord God said, It is not good that the man should be alone: I will make him an help meet for him."* (Genesis 2:18)

2. My husband is my second priority. This

important priority should never conflict with my first priority. If I have not met my husband's needs and taken the time to know him intimately, I do not have the right to take on another type of job or Christian service. My husband and I make each other a priority by setting aside some time for meaningful conversation each day and by scheduling an evening each week to do basically nothing but enjoy each other's company. I also make him a priority by caring for his home, meals and clothing. Therefore, good housekeeping as it is needed to meet the needs of my husband falls under my second priority. Taking care of my health and my appearance would also be a part of my number two priority. If I become obsessed with an immaculate home or a flawless appearance, I am revealing that they are out of their proper order. Last but not least, I make him a priority by supporting him in his purpose—doing the will of God for his life.

In establishing my third priority, I asked myself, "Who else is there in my life who is directly under my care?" My two children are the only ones at this time who have been placed in my home and directly under my care. *"Train up a child in the way He should go: and when he is old, he will not depart from it."* (Proverbs 22:6) The Bible has commanded me to teach and to train them.

3. My children are my third priority. I find that as a busy preacher's wife, I will not do many of the more important things if I do not schedule time for them. Because of a busy schedule, I have set time aside each day to be alone with my children, doing something they enjoy.

I believe discipline includes four aspects. They are (1) love, which to me includes talking, listening, touching, and playing; (2) schedule; (3) teaching; (4) punishment. Too often we think of discipline only as punishment. I believe that if we neglect to do the four parts of discipline, we have neglected our priorities.

In establishing my fourth priority, I asked myself, "Is there any other thing that God commands every Christian to do?" My answer came from Matthew 28:19-20. *"Go ye therefore, and teach all nations, baptizing them in the name of the Father, and of the Son, and of the Holy Ghost: Teaching them to observe all things whatsoever I have commanded you: and, lo, I am with you alway, even unto the end of the world."*

4. Soul winning is my fourth priority. I am not saying that soul winning is less important than the aforementioned, but I am saying that all four of these are so important that they are top priorities in my life. In fact, it is my belief that these four basic priorities are essential for a wife and mother to be a good Christian. Therefore, whenever I have had a time of transition in my life, I have tried to schedule these four priorities first. When there have been times that I have had to let things go in my life, these are the four things I have refused to let go. I can't get by without them.

When my son Kenny was born, for awhile I did not keep the house as clean as I would have liked. I was unable to keep all my responsibilities going in tip-top shape while recuperating from a Caesarean section. However, when Kenny was two weeks old, I took him to the nursery so I could go soul winning on my regularly scheduled day. I also began to leave him once a week with a baby-sitter so I could go on a date with my husband. I put him in the nursery during the church services so I could be by my husband's side in church. I did not feel guilty because I knew these were my priorities. I also took a year off from teaching to be home with Kenny much of the time because

I knew he was a very important priority.

I'm afraid that I was tempted to do just the opposite as a new mother. I wanted to keep the house immaculate, care for the baby, and just lay out of soul winning for a while. I was also sure that the Lord and my husband would understand if I didn't have time for them for a while. I would just be too exhausted, of course, with my duties and the baby and all. I'm afraid this schedule imbalance is part of the reason why new mothers suffer from what is called "postpartum blues." (I am sure in some cases that there are physical reasons, too.)

I tell the young students in my class that whenever they experience a transition, they need to immediately schedule time for their first priorities before they schedule time for anything else. Let me stress here that, after the first priorities are scheduled securely in a lady's life, she should add other responsibilities slowly. I believe it is better to add things too slowly than to add things quickly and then quit. Quitting is a bad habit!

In establishing my next priority, I asked myself, "Is there another area that should have a place in my schedule?" *"For God is not unrighteous to forget your work and labour of love, which ye have shewed toward his name, in that ye have ministered to the saints, and do minister."* (Hebrews 6:10)

5. My fifth priority is my Christian service. The importance of my Christian service differs according to how much commitment is involved. I am already committed to teach Thursday and Friday mornings at Hyles-Anderson College; therefore, my teaching would take priority over anything that might occur during this same time.

My Christian service that is a part of my local New Testament church would take priority over other

Christian service. My Sunday school class of nine girls at First Baptist Church of Hammond, Indiana, would take priority over my college classes of 150 girls. If I needed to discontinue something, I would quit teaching at the college before I would quit my Sunday school class.

A Christian wife should decide what Christian service should be included on her priority list by examining her desires and those of her husband and by examining the talents which God has given her. She should not choose her Christian service by comparing herself to other women and their abilities. *". . . but they measuring themselves by themselves, and comparing themselves among themselves, are not wise."* (II Corinthians 10:12)

For example, God has given me some ability in the area of teaching. My teaching takes precedence over other areas in which I am not as proficient. I make my decisions about where I should focus my time in my Christian service according to where I have the most ability.

Let me also say here that someone who is failing at priorities one through four should not take on a new type of Christian service until she is succeeding in the most important areas of her life.

In reviewing my priority list, I asked myself, "Are there others to whom I should give my time?" Philippians 2:4 teaches, *"Look not every man on his own things, but every man also on the things of others."*

"Others, Lord, Yes, Others"

6. My sixth priority is helping others. I am not saying that helping others is the least important thing in my life. Rather, I am saying that all my priorities are important. If helping others was not an important part of my life, it

would not be on my priority list at all. I include helping others by having a scheduled time in my week when I send out cards to the sick and the grieving of our church. I also send out cards of congratulations and appreciation at this time.

One reason I clip coupons and watch for sales is so I might have enough money left over after I have shopped for my own family to shop for others. Garage sales and thrift shops are good places where even poor people can afford to help others. I would advise every Christian lady to include money in her allowance or grocery money to give toward helping others. Another good practice would be to buy the same item for someone else whenever you buy an item for a family member. Honoring one's parents and being thoughtful of immediate family members is another way to make helping others a priority in our lives.

I realize that I have left out a few priorities that may be a part of someone's life even though they are not a part of mine. A career is one such example. I believe that an occupation would come either before or after Christian service, depending upon the reason for that job. A profession as a main source of income for the family would be a higher priority than one which is simply a tool for fulfillment.

I am not opposed to a woman working outside the home, but I do believe that it is always unwise for a woman to work only because of money. Some other reasoning should be involved. I am also convinced that the Bible teaches that the woman should be the main keeper of the home. This does not mean she cannot work, nor does it mean that her husband cannot help her around the house. However, I do believe that when a man becomes a "house husband," he and his wife have priorities that are contrary to the Bible. The wife should be the **main** keeper of the home.

A social life would also be a priority most women would have. Social life has never been an important priority in my life. My husband and I enjoy being close to the people who serve the Lord with us, and we find little time or need for social life. Still, we do enjoy some special friendships with other Christian couples. And there are times when our need to socialize becomes greater than at other times. At those times, socializing might become a higher priority in our lives. Most of the time, however, it falls below the above-stated priorities.

Remember, a woman can enjoy friendships and work simultaneously. One of my closest friends goes fruit and vegetable picking with me each year. Another close friend goes with me to thrift shops when I need to purchase something for my family or for others. Some of my dearest friends in all the world are my soul-winning partners.

So often the difference between a great lady and a good lady is simply a matter of priorities. Sad to say, priorities are often the simple difference between a great marriage and a bad marriage.

Let's not only do God's **will** as Christian wives; let's do it in God's **order** with proper priorities.

CHAPTER VI

Let's Build a Leader

"Let this mind be in you, which was also in Christ Jesus: Who, being in the form of God, thought it not robbery to be equal with God: But made himself of no reputation, and took upon him the form of a servant." (Philippians 2:5-7)

While I was a student in a Christian high school, the speakers in chapel often challenged me to love the Lord with all my soul, mind, strength, and body.   I often wondered back then how much I really did love God, and I felt saddened because I didn't even understand how to measure my love for Him.

I believe God understood how difficult it would be for a human being to express his love to Him. After all, God is a Spirit, and how does one show love to a Spirit? One way that my husband shows me his love is by buying me a Kit-Kat candy bar, which happens to be my favorite. But God doesn't have a favorite candy bar, and if He did, I'm not sure how I could send it to Him. I'm not sure how God would feel it if I gave Him a big hug, but I'm sure if I did, my friends would think I had lost my mind.

I used to believe that the best way to measure my love for God was by checking to see how loudly I groaned when I prayed, or how pious I looked when I was approaching God in prayer. As I have grown older, and I hope more spiritually mature, I have realized that love for God has little to do with these things.   Love is best measured through obedience. The most important obedience we can give is that which we give to our closest authority.

A child's most direct authority is his parents. So the best way for a child to show his love for God is by obeying his parents. *"Children, obey your parents in the Lord: for this is right."* (Ephesians 6:1) A man's best way to prove his love for God is by obeying his employer and by honoring his pastor. *"Servants, obey in all things your masters according to the flesh; not with eyeservice, as menpleasers; but in singleness of heart, fearing God."* (Colossians 3:22) A wife's best way to show her love for God is by obeying her husband. *"Wives, submit yourselves unto your own husbands, as unto the Lord."* (Ephesians 5:22)

Some of us think God is rather ignorant and easy to fool. We prove this when we get in our prayer closet, tell God that we love Him, then get up and argue with our husband while selfishly demanding our own way. Yet the truth is, God is neither ignorant nor easy to fool. He knows the truth about our love for Him, not by what we say in our prayer time, but rather by how we treat the most direct authority that He has placed in our lives—our husbands.

I like to say, "I told you so." I know these words are not pleasing to very many people. However, the one time when I **can** say, "I told you so," is when I get on my knees and tell God I love Him then submit to my husband's wishes, even when we disagree. It is at these times when I can look to Heaven and say to Jesus,

"I told You so. I told You I loved You,
and I just proved it with my life."

An Exciting Challenge

This is the first and main reason why I see submission as an exciting challenge. I even view submission as the most exciting part of God's marriage plan. I enjoy speaking about it and writing about it more than any other subject. Why? Because submission to my husband is my best way to show God that I love Him. Submission is a woman's way of saying to God, "I told You so. I told You I loved You, and I just proved it."

If my husband and I never disagreed about anything or if I never had to give in to him, I would never have a chance to show God how much I really do love Him. Therefore, disagreements provide us with an opportunity to display our love for Christ. Submission to our husbands is our great measuring stick for love, and there is no way we can get around it. We cannot be improperly related to our husbands, yet be kind to our neighbor, pastor, and others and say that we are right with God. Our husbands are the best receivers of our love for God, and there is no way of getting around this fact.

One of the reasons many people are offended by the word "submission" is because they fail to recognize the challenge and opportunity it brings for showing our love for our Creator. Another reason many folks do not appreciate submission is their misunderstanding of what biblical submission really is. Therefore, I would like to share three statements regarding what submission is **not**.

1. Submission is not slavery. Princess Diana of Wales is not a slave by any stretch of the imagination. Yet British law requires her to walk a given number of paces behind her husband at some public appearances. I am not

sure whether this law is obeyed, but it remains a fact that Princess Diana's position is inferior to that of her husband. However, none of us would consider this modern-day princess a slave. Why? Because she is a queen with her own throne. This same thing can be said of the submissive Christian wife. She, too, has her own throne and can rule as a queen. A woman's throne (or power) is influence whereas a man's throne is leadership. Who is to say which is the greatest power? Who is the greatest—the man who leads our country as president, or the woman who influences the man who leads our country? I think this is one of those questions I am going to ask God when we reach Heaven. I'm afraid I won't know the answer until then. Nevertheless, each partner in the marriage relationship has his own throne.

- A man's throne is leadership.
- A woman's throne is influence.

An obvious fact can be assumed about someone who is trying to get on another's throne: that person has left his own throne. This is the case with the so-called liberated woman. As she tries to get on man's throne of leadership, she loses her position on her own throne of influence. Let me restate this another way.

- When a woman takes leadership, she loses influence.
- When a woman gives leadership, she gains influence.

Probably the most influential wife of a president of the United States during my lifetime has been Mrs. Nancy Reagan. She was often criticized for the strong impact she made on her husband's leadership decisions. I do not believe it is any coincidence that this same woman was also criticized for making such statements as, "Ronnie is my whole life." I believe she was the most influential first lady because she gave complete loyalty and leadership to her husband. When a woman gives such leadership to her husband and allows him to take a number one role in her life, he is motivated. **Nothing motivates a man like leadership.** When a husband is motivated by his wife, he turns to her for influence. The best way to influence a husband is through encouragement.

In any institution, one person must ultimately be in charge. This is true of any church, school, or corporation. This is also true of any marriage. It is just as silly for two people to try to run a home as it is for two people to drive a car. Ask any recently licensed driver how it works when mom tries to "help" him drive from the back seat. Usually, this does more harm than good, and sometimes causes collisions. The same is true when a marriage has a wife as a back-seat driver. This often causes marital conflict resulting in a collision that wounds not only the husband, but also the children in the back seat.

True Submission

In John 13:3-5, there is an account of Jesus doing a very submissive task. *"Jesus knowing that the Father had given all things into his hands, and that he was come from God, and went to God; He riseth from supper, and laid aside his garments; and took a towel, and girded himself. After that he poureth water into a bason, and began to wash the disciples' feet, and to wipe them with the towel wherewith he was girded."*

However, none of us thinks of Jesus as a slave. Why?

Because He volunteered to serve. **When we are forced to serve, we are slaves. When we volunteer to serve, we are servants.** The Bible teaches us that to be a servant is the highest calling of all: *"But he that is greatest among you shall be your servant."* (Matthew 23:11)

Why was Jesus able to volunteer to do such a menial task? I believe that John 13:3 gives us an explanation. This verse directly precedes the story of Jesus washing the disciples' feet. *"Jesus knowing that the Father had given all things into his hands, and that he was come from God and went to God."* This verse tells us that Jesus could do this task because He knew who He was. In other words, He had a good sense of identity or self-worth. Jesus' identity could be found in His position as Christ, and this is also where we can find our identity as Christians. When we understand our identity, we will not only understand the true meaning of the word *meekness,* but we will cease to be offended by the deeds of submission. When we accepted Jesus Christ into our hearts, our position became very similar to that of Christ's. To understand this concept better, let's examine exactly how Jesus' identity was described in John 13:3.

Identity A. Jesus knew that the Father had given all things into His hands. Everything that belonged to God the Father also belonged to Jesus, so why should anyone or anything have intimidated **Him?** Yet the Bible clearly teaches that all that belongs to God is also available to every one of His children. Now we obviously do not all have the same amount of money in the bank. Some of our wealth has not been claimed by us yet. It is also likely that some of our inheritance is being held by our Father until later when we will be better able to enjoy it. Yet we all truly possess all things in Christ. How foolish for us to look down on someone who has less money in his savings account.

Identity B. Jesus knew that He was come from God. Well, from where in the world do you think we came? The story of our creation by God Himself is given to us in the book of Genesis, Psalm 139, and many other places in the Bible.

Identity C. Jesus knew He was going back to God. Knowing that He was God's Son and that He would soon be ascending to Heaven to be with His Father again, Jesus did not only feel able to submit to washing the disciples' feet, but He was also able to submit to the mocking, jeering, and persecution of others as He died on the cross. We Christians are also soon to be ascending into Heaven. Because of Jesus' example, we should not be intimidated by the most submissive of tasks, which is ultimately the cross of death to self.

To me, John 13:3 is the best verse in the Bible depicting meekness. When we understand the position of every believer, we will never again be so foolish as to look down upon one of our brothers or sisters in Christ nor will we feel inferior to others. We will also be able to serve our fellow man in the most ungratifying ways without feeling that our self-value is somehow being threatened.

2. Submission is not suppression. Many people have the misconception that a submissive wife will never speak her opinion when it is in disagreement with that of her husband. To the contrary, if a wife is to be a helpmeet for her husband, there will be times when she must express disagreement to complete him spiritually and otherwise. This is always to be handled in a wise and biblical manner, yet it is a necessity even for a submissive Christian wife.

3. Submission is not being a doormat. Many a

woman feels that if she submits to her husband's authority, he will be motivated to walk all over her emotions. Just the opposite is true. A man who is given leadership by his wife is motivated to cherish her and to care for her as a *"weaker vessel."* *"Likewise, ye husbands, dwell with them according to knowledge, giving honour unto the wife, as unto the weaker vessel, as being heirs together of the grace of life; that your prayers be not hindered."* (I Peter 3:7)

No Resistance

Now that I have shared what submission is **not,** I would like to share what submission **is.** I could give you a lengthy definition of submission. I have read many in my studies through the years. Yet it is difficult for me to remember these definitions, especially when I am being less than submissive toward my husband. Consequently, I have coined a two-word definition for the word *submission.*

Submission = No Resistance

If you can remember the feeling you had the last time you heard someone scrape his fingernails down a chalkboard, you can understand the feeling of resistance. It is the same feeling a wife has when her husband asks her to do something she does not wish to do. I am not saying that a submissive wife will never have this resistant feeling; I **am** saying that when she does feel it, she will not hang onto it, but will let it go.

I realize as a Christian that everything God allows in my life, He works together for good. *"And we know that all things work together for good to them that love God, to them who are the called according to his purpose."*

(Romans 8:28) Therefore, if I live by faith, I will not feel any resistance toward my husband. Instead, I will place my trust in God, breathe a sigh of relief, and let go of my resistance while yielding to my husband's will.

Now that we have learned a good definition for submission, let us examine what else submission is.

1. Submission is a command from God. Though we should be motivated by this fact alone, many of us are not. The reason probably is because it is the only explanation we have heard. However, it is an accurate explanation. Ephesians 5:22 says, *"Wives, submit yourselves unto your own husbands, as unto the Lord."* God's commands are unchanged by our husbands' moods and inclinations. Submission is therefore unconditional. The Bible clearly reveals that the man is the head of the woman and that the woman was made in the image of man. Submission in marriage is God's plan. As I have grown older, I seem to learn more and more that when God plans something, He plans it for the good of all who are involved. This leads us to our next point.

2. Submission is necessary for a wife's happiness and freedom. When I was sixteen, I became a licensed driver. I was an extremely independent sixteen-year-old. Perhaps that is the reason why the day I first received my license, I drove by myself down the expressway for a couple of hours just reveling in my independence.

Today I am thirty-one, and I do not revel in my independence as much. You see, I now am a wife, a housekeeper, a cook, a laundress, and a mother of two children. Add to this the fact that I am a Sunday school teacher, a part-time college faculty member, a speaker, and a writer. I could add to that list, and most women in their thirties or over could add to theirs also. As I gained more responsibilities, I lost much of my desire for independence. That desire has been replaced by a need to lean upon someone else for my strength.

Most women find that this same change of desire takes place in their hearts, too. Age and responsibility seem to create a weariness that longs for emotional leadership and support. The problem is that most women do not realize this until it is too late. A woman will lead the family and the home until she tires of it. When she grows weary of leading, she looks to her husband to take over. Having lacked practice, he is unable to satisfy his wife's need for a strong leader. She then oftentimes despises him. Thus, I view submission as a challenge for me to build in my husband what I will respect and need as I grow older. A stubborn young man will be a rock of Gibraltar when health problems set in years from now.

Isn't God good to plan such a sweet gift for His female creation? He gives us the opportunity to build in our husbands what we need by our very obedience. He causes it to pay off in the sweet reward of strength at the time in our lives when we will need it most. Surely God loves females.

3. Submission is a husband's God-designed need. Some ladies believe their husbands are brute beasts because they become "bullies" when their leadership is threatened. Yet God has called the husband to be the head of the home. When God calls someone to do something, He also gives him the desire and the ability to do it. Henceforth, it is normal for a man to desire leadership and to feel emasculated when his leadership is threatened. I would worry if my husband did not feel enraged when bossed by me.

4. Submission is necessary for the rearing of good

children. Your children will be as obedient as you are. That is a scary thought, yet an accurate one. Let me share with you a silly story to help illustrate this point.

One November several years ago, I was getting ready to leave to teach at Hyles-Anderson College. I was going to take Jaclynn to her regular baby-sitter and then go to the college. As we were walking out the door, I told my daughter she needed to wear her coat. It was one of the first chilly days of late autumn, and Jaclynn was not willing to put on her coat. I explained to her that she would have to obey her mother and put on her coat. She agreed to put it on, but proceeded to tell me that she would not be willing to zip it. I persuaded her to zip her coat, and all was well—that is, until my husband called to me saying he felt I needed to wear a coat also.

I did not have a nice winter coat at the time and was embarrassed to wear the one I had. So I told him I wasn't going to wear a coat. I again headed for the door. On my way to the door, I noticed my daughter was looking at me with her big brown eyes in a very questioning manner. I knew then that I must go back to the closet and put on my coat in submission to my husband.

Would I have been a rebellious wife had I not put on that coat? Probably not! But I would have missed a wonderful opportunity to teach my child about submission.

Children do many things to find out who is in charge in their home, and they **do know** who is in charge. It is important, then, that a wife do all she can to transfer the leadership when her husband arrives home from work. I give it my best effort to see that my husband makes all the decisions for our children when he is at home.

5. Submission avoids conflicts. Several years ago, while sitting in an evening service at First Baptist Church of

Hammond, I observed something very interesting. A couple came into the service late and began looking for a seat. The wife found a seat and turned into a row that was about five pews ahead of our family. The husband did not see his wife sit down, and he continued to walk down the aisle looking for a seat. He finally found one and sat down about ten rows ahead of us. Of course, when he sat down, he discovered something very shocking. His wife was not beside him! He then turned around and found her sitting five rows behind him. He began to motion to her to join him. She shook her head "no." She then began to motion for him to join her. This went on for several minutes. I must admit that I had stopped listening to the announcements being given at the time. I was being entertained by what was going on between this man and woman. Finally, the husband (with a very red face) walked back five rows and joined his wife.

I do not believe this incident proved that this wife was rebellious. However, rebellious or not, she made her husband look and feel foolish. I realize this was only a minor conflict of desires, but it is a good illustration of how submission avoids conflicts. After all, what was he to do? He couldn't continue to motion to his wife during the entire service. Neither could he go back and get her and drag her down the aisle.

In any situation when a wife is not willing to yield her will to her husband, he has no good choice but to yield to her.

The husband is supposed to be the head of the wife. Therefore, when his wife does not give him leadership, he is forced to act in a way which is contrary to God's Word. That is to say, he has two choices.

- He can choose to be a bully. He can demand leadership by use of cruelty or force.
- He can choose to be a wimp. He can allow his wife to lead.

Neither of these are good choices. Nobody likes a bully. It is not Christlike to bully someone into followship. Nevertheless, as much as I dislike a bully, I dislike a wimp even more. It is against Bible principles for a husband to be led by his wife.

The only **good** solution is for the wife to **give** leadership to her husband and to follow him. This allows him to be the leader God intended him to be without having to behave in an unchristlike manner.

Ephesians 5:21 says, *"Submitting yourselves one to another in the fear of God."* Yet verse 23 of the same chapter tells us that *". . . the husband is the head of the wife . . ."* How can these two Bible principles be reconciled? By both yielding their wills to each other. However, the wife should be the greater yielder.

If it is decided ahead of time who will get his way when there is a difference of opinion regarding a seat in church, conflict and embarrassment will be avoided. Submission avoids conflict in every area of a marriage. If submission is not used to solve the little conflicts in marriage, neither will it be used to solve major ones.

6. Submission is the oil that keeps the machinery of marriage running smoothly. When I began to study for the Christian Wife class I teach, I became excited about the subject of submission. I decided then to think of as many ways as possible, big and small, that I could give leadership to my husband. When I began to act submissively, he began

to value me more and ask my advice. He treated me better than he ever had before. This made me want to give more leadership, which in turn made him want to have more of my influence. The cycle has continued on and on, running very smoothly. That is exactly how God intended a marriage to run—very smoothly.

Many couples never get off the starting block as far as submission is concerned because they want the other person in the marriage to start. It is my belief that the marriage machine **must** start with the wife's **giving** submission to her husband. Remember, submission is not obeying a man's demand; it is a woman's *gift* to her husband.

Submission causes a man to feel responsible. When a wife says to her husband, "Anything you can do, I can do better," she takes away his responsibility. I believe that is why we have in our society so many husbands who simply do not come home. They work from 9 to 5, and then go to the health club or to the bar. Home is only a place to sleep. They do not participate in the child rearing process. Why? Because wives have not given them leadership.

As stated previously, leadership motivates and causes a man to feel responsible. He then will be more prone to take part in the responsibilities of the home, the marriage, and the family. Let me break this down into three points:

- A woman begins the process by giving leadership.
- A man is motivated and feels responsible so he asks for his wife's help.
- A woman feels important and cherished, so she gives more leadership.

This cycle could repeat itself over and over again. When the Bible concept of submission is followed, the wife's desire to give leadership just increases while the husband just becomes more motivated and increasingly appreciative of his wife's virtues.

My hope is that, somewhere in this chapter, you have become as excited about the concept of leadership as I am. Allow me to repeat myself when I say that leadership is not giving in to a husband's demand; rather, it is a wife's *gift* to her husband. This gift has some rewards in it for a wife in that it prepares her husband to be the strength she will need and respect as she grows older. It also has rewards for the husband as it prepares him to lead successfully in other areas of his life. In other words, God planned submission and God plans all things for the good of everyone involved, children included.

What a good God we have! Let's praise Him for His wonderful plan, and let's go forth to build a leader.

CHAPTER VII

Romance

"I am my beloved's, and my beloved is mine . . ."
(Song of Solomon 6:3)

Anyone who has read the book of Song of Solomon realizes that romance is biblical. Proverbs 5 also reminds us that romance is not only biblical, but important. Few are the women who would not willingly admit that having some sort of romance in their marriage is important to them personally. Many of these same women probably would have to admit that their marriage relationship suffers romantically. In the following paragraphs, I would like to share some principles that should motivate a woman to put priority on the romantic aspect of her marriage.

Principles of Romance

1. Realize it is not what you have, but what you do with what you have that is important. Many wives would say something like this, "I really am an affectionate person, and I would express it if I could only lose ten pounds. My problem is, I just don't feel good about myself."

I'm afraid that is not the problem at all. We would put more priority upon romance and just being affectionate in general if we realized that we either are affectionate or unaffectionate people. In other words, if you are not an affectionate wife now, you will never be affectionate. You would not be affectionate if you had a perfect figure; neither would you be affectionate if you had the perfect husband and the perfect circumstances. You are simply not an affectionate person.

I realize that I am being rather hard on women when I make that statement. I know there are times in all our lives when illness, temporary depression, or another physical problem causes us to be less loving than we would ordinarily be. However, to be the husband of an unloving wife is a tragedy. It is no less a tragedy to be a wife who is unable to give love to her husband. The best way to motivate ourselves to be otherwise is to realize that lack of affection is a condition of the heart. It is not our bodies that need to change so much; nor is it our husbands. It is our hearts and attitudes.

The famous actress Cher does a commercial in which she advertises a particular health club. In this advertisement she says something like this: "If you want a body like this, you have to work out." There are several things about this commercial that I find humorous. First, it is public knowledge that Cher paid a high price for whatever kind of body she has. Secondly, Cher has been married and divorced more than once, so if a perfect body is the answer, she obviously needs to work out some more.

One day I realized that I have something Cher does not have. I enjoy making this statement about her to my class at the college. Each semester the students look at me as though they are having a hard time understanding what that something could be. In case you too are baffled, I will share with you what it is.

I have a happy and affectionate relationship with the first and only man I ever plan to marry. If I were rich enough, I suppose I could have enough cosmetic surgeries to make me completely satisfied with myself. If I had a little more time, perhaps I could work out until I fulfilled the world's standard of bodily perfection. Yet if I have not taken the time to learn how to share myself with my husband, then I am no different from a perfectly painted China doll and deserve to be left standing on the shelf.

I am not saying that we should let ourselves go physically. We should do what we can to make ourselves an attractive mate for our husband's delight. I **am** saying, however, that a good Christian husband would often give his right arm just to have a wife who is willing to share her love with him.

2. Realize your romance cannot be measured by what it used to be nor by what you intend it to be. A woman is not an affectionate wife because she was affectionate five years ago. Nor is she affectionate because she has always intended to be. I'm afraid the reason our relationships oftentimes do not improve is because we tend to see ourselves in light of what we used to do or in light of what we intend to do rather than in light of what we are doing now.

3. Realize that romance was not just designed by God for men. Romance is a woman's best friend. God designed the physical relationship to be a protection from temptation for **both** spouses. Proverbs 6:26 tells us that *"the adulteress will hunt for the precious life."*

My husband is as pure and godly a man as I have ever known. Because he is used of God in many special ways, I realize he could be that precious life referred to in Proverbs 6. That is to say, I am sure the devil would like to place some type of irresistible temptation in his pathway. First Corinthians 10:13 tells us that with every temptation God has provided a way of escape. *"There hath no temptation taken you but such as is common to man: but God is faithful, who will not suffer you to be tempted above that ye are able; but will with the temptation also make a way to escape, that ye may be able to bear it."* One way of escaping immorality is explained in Proverbs 5:18 where the young man is encouraged to *". . . rejoice with the wife of thy youth."* Therefore, I believe God designed romance with the woman in mind also. The sexual relationship in marriage protects each spouse from temptation and saves them only for each other.

Because the marriage relationship is to picture the love that exists between Christ and the church, every part of the marriage should be exciting and enthusiastic. *"Husbands, love your wives, even as Christ also loved the church, and gave himself for it."* (Ephesians 5:25) When we see Christ in Heaven someday, it will be an exciting time. Even those of us who are introverts will become lost in the thrill of seeing Him face to face. It is my belief that every aspect of the marriage, including the romantic aspect, should depict not only the love, but the joy and enthusiasm of the love that exists between Christ and the church.

4. Realize it is the woman's responsibility to keep the romance alive. Perhaps if I were writing a book entitled, *The Christian Husband,* I would approach the topic of romance differently. Still, I am not sure that I would. Why? Because, generally speaking, it is harder – or shall I say more complicated – for a woman to be responsive than it is for a man.

A man can easily become responsive in a messy house, but a woman often cannot. She needs certain conditions to be right. My theory is that if a woman needs certain conditions, she should create those conditions. She may say, "My husband should take the responsibility in creating the right conditions for romance." Perhaps he should, but sometimes we wives are pretty difficult to figure out. No one else understands what we need quite like we do ourselves. If we truly care about loving our husbands, we will find out what those needs are and set about having the conditions right for romance.

I'm afraid there are many wives who run to the altar on a regular basis praying that the Lord will give them a more affectionate heart, then return to their seats and to their homes unchanged. There is an old adage that says, "The Lord helps those who help themselves." I consider this to be true in many ways in the area of romance. **While we are praying that the Lord will make us affectionate wives**, we should also be doing the little practical things that will cause a response in us. **Lack of romance is most often a practical problem rather than a spiritual problem.** All the praying in the world will not cure the problem if we are unwilling to do the thoughtful deeds that cause love to thrive in a marriage.

Now that we have established that there are some things that are necessary in order for romance to thrive in a marriage, let us discuss what those things are.

Successful Romance

• Romance needs beautiful surroundings. Several years ago, before my husband and I moved into the house in which we now live, I looked around at my surroundings in my home and decided that they were not conducive to romance. That day, I vowed that I was going to make some changes in my home environment. From that day until now, I have tried to make the most important consideration when decorating my home to be that of the relationship between myself and my husband.

I am not much of a television viewer, much less a soap opera fan, yet I am sure that when a soap opera shows an illicit affair, it does not show it in a garbage dump. Rather, it probably shows the wickedness in a beautiful bedroom decorated like a picture from a *Better Homes and Gardens* magazine. Why? Because romance needs pretty surroundings to survive.

I am well aware that most of those who read this book cannot afford to decorate like *Better Homes and Gardens*. Perhaps you are a newlywed and just inherited the couch Uncle Fred died on. You may wish to replace it, but you probably cannot afford to do so. I would like to share some ideas for having beautiful surroundings on a limited income.

First, I would strongly encourage any new bride who is working with limited funds to start with just one area of her house or apartment and decorate it with romance in mind. Perhaps this area would be the master bedroom. You may scrimp and save as you decorate the other areas of your home. However, only buy for your "special area" what you think is truly beautiful. It still does not have to be expensive. I prefer pinching pennies even in my "special area." However, I would not settle for something that did not suit my taste in this particular area.

When I say to decorate in a way that is conducive to romance, I am not speaking about red satin pillows and suggestive posters on the walls. This type of decor would be offensive to guests, and most women would not find these surroundings to make them responsive at all. I am suggesting that you decorate your "special area" in a way you find to be beautiful.

When I think of something conducive to romance, I

think of bright and cheerful shades of color and floral prints. Perhaps you would not agree. Go with your taste. What you think about it is what is important.

I have also found that playing beautiful music can make a dull atmosphere seem 100 percent more romantic. Lighting even a small candle can change my whole attitude and the attitudes of those around me. Boiling a bit of potpourri on the stove can affect me tremendously. I don't feel very romantic when my house smells like day-old garbage.

Often when I call to tell my mother that I am stopping by her house for a few moments to pick up something, I notice that she has lighted a candle or turned on some potpourri to make me feel welcome. Because I am a woman, I always notice. You see, my surroundings affect me tremendously, and your surroundings affect you also. So, let's create those right surroundings.

I hope you are understanding the difference that occurs when you greet your husband after a busy day after having started some beautiful music, lighted a few candles, and warmed some potpourri on the stove. It prevents his arrival from being an afterthought and prepares you to be pleasant when you greet him at the door. To be prepared for a pleasant greeting need not take a great amount of time. However, it does take more than we often are willing to give.

• Romance needs fun times. If I could only write one paragraph on how to have a happy marriage, included in that paragraph would be this advice: Have a date night. My husband and I were advised to have a date night before we were even married. When we first married, we sometimes wondered why we even had one. You see, in the early years of our marriage, my husband got home from work at 1:00 in the afternoon. We continued to go through the ritual of the Friday night date. Now, twelve years later, I am so glad that we did. Because of his increasingly busy schedule, I sometimes barely get to see him at all until Friday night rolls around. Friday is our time to become reacquainted, and what precious memories we have of these special times.

There are many things a couple can do on their date night. I believe that simply to eat out at a restaurant is the best plan. Why? Because when you are eating, you have to talk. Have you ever noticed how awkward it feels to be sitting with someone at a restaurant and not be able to think of anything to say? The restaurant does not need to be expensive. Often through the years, we have met at the local coffee shop that is just a five-minute drive from our home. We have sat and talked for an hour over nothing but a cup of coffee because that was really all we could afford. Then we hurried home when our hour was up so we wouldn't go broke paying the baby-sitter. Our happiest memories are those simple talks over coffee.

I also believe in making birthdays and holidays as traditional and exciting as possible. Jack often says to me, "I would marry you all over just for the fun you make of the holidays." There really does not need to be a holiday in order for a fun time to be planned. When a wife is having a hard time being responsive or the romance in her marriage has lost its lustre, she should get off her chair and plan a fun time.

• Romance needs courtesy. Have you ever wondered why our culture practices chivalry? It really is quite humorous. When a woman reaches a door at the same time that a man does, she is expected to let him open it. When she reaches a door by herself, she is perfectly capable of opening it herself. Yet every time my husband opens a door for me, carries a package, or helps me with my coat, he is reminding me of something very important—that I am a lady. Please excuse my frankness, but in essence he is saying through his actions, "Hey, hey, Baby! I'm a man, and you're a lady. What do you want to do about it?" He is reminding me of our differences—his strength versus my weakness. It is our differences that create in us a need for romance.

That difference is why the Equal Rights movement has not improved our divorce rate but has caused more deterioration. When a man and woman are too much alike, they are no longer attracted to each other romantically. If I arrive home with ten bags of groceries, I may be capable of carrying them in the house while my husband watches television. (Just for the record, there is little chance of that happening.) Still, I can carry all the bags myself and not be any the worse for it. However, I would be unwise. If I want to have a romantic relationship, I must act like a lady and allow my husband to be a leader and a gentleman.

• Romance needs touch. I am talking here about taking advantage of the little moments. It is rare for me to pass my husband without giving him a quick pat on the back or another nonsexual gesture of affection. Touch directly affects a man's self-confidence and his job performance. It also prepares both spouses for romance.

• Romance needs verbal and written expression. I almost never hang up the phone or leave my husband's presence without saying, "I love you." He also does the same. This practice was carried out in my home when I was growing up and has also become habit in my own home. Rarely a week goes by that I do not at some time express to my husband in writing that I love and appreciate him. I do this most often through some type of silly card that I picked up at the grocery store. Romance needs verbal and written expression to survive.

- Last, but not least, romance needs a challenge. When Jack and I were dating, I used to wonder how a man could be married to one woman all his life and not become tired of her. Sometimes when I thought he might be tired of me, I would even express a desire to break up and date around. I did not do this because I really wanted to break up. I did it to be sure I was still a challenge to my boyfriend.

Once, however, he got smart and decided to take me up on my offer. When I saw him the next day, I let him know that I had not really meant what I said. I quickly learned that I was going about being a challenge to my boyfriend in the wrong way. It is important that even the most mature of relationships contain some sort of challenge—but the right kind of challenge. We can be the right kind of challenge to our spouses by doing two things.

The Right Kind of Challenge

First, find your joy in the Lord. Psalms 37:4 says, *"Delight thyself also in the Lord; and he shall give thee the desires of thine heart."*

As I mentioned in a previous chapter, for the first few years after my husband started traveling, I was very sad and lonely during his absence. I spent much of my time grieving his departure and looking forward to his return. Yet, the strangest thing would happen when he did return. I found that I did not feel like rejoicing at all. Instead, I was whiny and the opposite of what a challenge should be. My problem was that I was trying to find joy in my husband instead of in the Lord. Because of trying to find my joy in my husband, I began to weigh my husband down to the point that I am not sure what he dreaded most—leaving me or having to come back to me again. But this cycle all changed one night when I decided to change my behavior. From that day until now, I have continued the process of learning how to find my joy only in the Lord.

Marriage is not for obtaining joy; rather it is for sharing a joy that we already possess. To know a person who possesses this kind of joy and serenity is to know a person who is truly a challenge. My husband is just such a person. He has a deep and consistent walk with the Lord Jesus Christ. I have no doubt that he loves Jesus far more than he loves me. This deep love is to my benefit. His relationship with the Lord has made him a person of great depth. I have known him for fourteen years and feel that I have barely scratched the surface of all the things there are to know about Jack Schaap. Fourteen years later, I have not even begun to tire of him. I am continually challenged by the privilege of getting to know him better.

Another way to be the right kind of challenge to your husband is to maintain that quality that first attracted him to you. Every wife should be aware of just what that quality is. It is usually some kind of youthful quality. For example, my husband has shared with me several times that what attracted him to me after our first date was my casual and unsophisticated way of making him feel comfortable. Fun-loving is another word that he has used often in describing his attraction to me.

As I grow older and have more responsibility, I find that being fun-loving does not come as easily. However, I put priority on maintaining this quality because I am aware of how important it is to him. As a woman gets older, she oftentimes ceases to be the person she was when she "caught" her husband. Perhaps she was expressive, thoughtful, carefree, and fun-loving at one time. Now she is practical, serious, and unaffectionate. In fact, she may not be the person to whom he was first attracted at all.

I am not suggesting that a married woman should remain immature. However, there is a part of me that does not wish to mature past the point of having a romantic relationship. A woman is the right kind of challenge to her husband when she strives to maintain some of the same qualities she had when she "caught" him. She now needs to maintain these qualities to "keep" him interested.

In closing, let me say that a wife should never look at her husband and then respond with the words, "Well, old Harold just doesn't turn me on anymore." Rather, she needs to realize the problem of an unaffectionate relationship lies within her heart. She must get her attitude right with Christ and with her husband. Then she must set about doing all the little practical things that will cause her to have the romantic relationship about which she has always dreamed.

Let's keep the home fires burning!

CHAPTER VIII

Discussing A Problem

*"Wherefore, my beloved brethren, let every man
be swift to hear, slow to speak, slow to wrath."*
(James 1:19)

When I was studying to teach the course upon which this book is based, I came across a startling statistic: over 75 percent of those people involved in fatal accidents had just concluded an argument. This discovery was an effective reminder of the destructiveness of bad conflict.

However, good conflict can be beneficial to a marriage. I believe one secret to Jack's and my marriage is our ability to discuss our differences and then to resolve them.

Some people believe that it is not submissive for a wife to express her differences of opinion to her husband. I believe that this very thing could be the key to a successful marriage if the differences are expressed properly. I would like to share some practical pointers on how to discuss problems properly.

Practical Pointers

1. Always pray about a problem before you discuss it with your husband. This measure will prevent you from losing your temper and arguing with him at an inappropriate time or place. It also will allow time for the physical mood or pressure that may have caused the

problem to pass. A couple should never quarrel in public, and praying first will prevent this from occurring.

After I pray about a particular problem, the Lord often assures me that it is just not worth discussing. Some of the time, however, He assures me that it would be best if I take the problem to my husband.

Another good determining factor when deciding whether to discuss a problem is for the wife to ask herself, "Does this problem occur on a regular basis?" We all make terrible mistakes now and then. We say things we should not say, do things we should not do. If a wife feels offended about something her husband did or said that is rare and out of character for him, it is usually best not to discuss it.

2. Set aside a time to discuss the problem with him. If a problem is worth discussing, it is worth setting up an appointment for discussion. Following this principle will prevent you from greeting him at the door with problems and from igniting his temper because the timing is not right.

After allowing at least 24 hours to pass (and preferably longer), then go to him and ask him if you can spend some time with him so you can receive help for a particular problem.

Your approach should be kind and non-threatening. Many wives say, "I need to talk to you" in a way that could drive any husband straight out of town. A wife must remember that even in discussing a problem with her husband, she does not have to tear him down. She can always build him up.

A time for discussion should be set. This should not be when either spouse will be tired or hungry. I also recommend that the discussion not take place on a date night, especially if it is serious in nature. A date night should be a time when both enjoy each other's company, not a time of dragging out problems and bringing dread.

3. If a wife is discussing an offense with her husband, her goal should be to understand why he has offended her. Usually when we argue with someone, our goal is to prove our point or to show the other person how hurt we really are. Neither of these is a good goal. If we are trying to prove our point, we will never resolve the problem. If we are trying to show how hurt we are, we must realize that no one will ever understand our hurt feelings adequately except Jesus Christ. However, once we understand why someone has done something, he can never hurt us in that same way again.

For example, one semester in my Christian Wife class, I had a student who was rebellious and unresponsive. Most of those in my class are top-notch students who are very interested in the subject material, so this type of behavior is very rare. It just so happened that I knew something about the difficulties this student had faced in her home life. This background information helped me to understand her seemingly negative attitude about the class. Because I understood her behavior, she did not hurt my feelings.

Suppose your husband is grouchy at a particular time of each day. Don't you think it would be better for you to understand why rather than try to prove to him how negatively his behavior affects you? When a wife is trying to understand her husband, she will not place blame and try to prove that the problem is her husband's fault.

4. State your feelings with love. Always include lots of love and praise as you "argue" with your husband. Avoid using the words *always* and *never*. Men are strange in that they think **never** means **never**. Women are more

intelligent; they realize that **never** does not mean never! If a wife says to her husband, "You never spend any time with me," he will try to prove that some time in the history of mankind he did spend time with her. Avoid saying things to him like, "You have the same problem." (You did the same thing three months ago.) Never say, "I told you so" or words with a similar meaning. (And there are **many** ways to say, "I told you so.")

Never use ridicule or condemnation when discussing a problem with your husband. Instead of saying something like, "You never spend any time with me," say something like, "I may be wrong, but I feel that I need more time with you." Both statements make the same point except one tears down and the other builds.

5.   A wife should allow her husband to react. Because most women are more emotional in nature, they feel they have a right to express their feelings and do so frequently. However, those same women will walk out of a room, slam the door, and not speak if their husbands express some sort of negative feelings to them. No wonder there are many expressionless, uncaring husbands in our society.

A wife should remember that it is a compliment when her husband feels free to express his feelings, especially if they are negative. He is trusting her to respond maturely and she should do exactly that. If she has a right to express criticism, he has that same right, too. When one expresses criticism, he or she should prepare for reaction, and should "take it like a man," so to speak. A wife must not only allow her husband to react to her complaints, but she must also avoid defending herself.

6.   A wife should not respond improperly to her husband's reaction. There are basically three inappropriate

reactions to use when discussing a problem: (1) explosion; (2) silence; (3) tears. Most of us are aware that to explode by throwing a vase or losing one's temper is wrong and sinful. However, the silent and tearful reactions are just as sinful. The silent treatment will cause anguish and health problems for both parties involved. Any of these reactions cause a man to receive the message that he can discuss his feelings with his wife only up to a certain point. Tears are a beautiful part of a woman, but they should not be used in arguments. When a wife cries over the hurts of others, her tears should move her husband to compassion. When she cries over herself and uses her tears as a weapon in an argument, he will become hardened to those tears.

7. A wife should see to it that the discussion ends when both parties agree that it should. In other words, when you open a discussion, you have no right to suddenly leave the room shouting, "I don't want to talk about it anymore!" It is not fair to express your feelings and then not allow your husband to do the same thing.

On the other hand, when he expresses his need to "cool down" before discussing the problem any further, you should trust him. Don't continue the conversation and cause him to reach his breaking point. Sometimes a wife will use Ephesians 4:26, *"Let not the sun go down upon your wrath"* as an excuse to pursue an argument that is going nowhere. I believe the best way to accomplish this biblical admonition— *"Let not the sun go down upon your wrath"*—is to get on your knees and ask God to take away your anger. This verse does not mean we have to carry on a meaningless conversation in exhaustion while we fruitlessly seek to find a solution. If you feel a need to end a conversation when he does not, you may say something like, "I'm beginning to understand your point of view. Can

I think about it for awhile?"

8. A wife should say, "I'm sorry," then genuinely forgive. Don't mention the argument again unless both parties have previously agreed to do so.

In closing, let me mention another key to having the right kind of conflict. Keep a sense of humor in the arguments. Of course, it would be inappropriate to laugh in your spouse's face when he expresses his problem. Still, I believe many a problem could be solved much better and sooner if both partners learn to laugh at themselves.

Most problems are not as serious as they seem; or perhaps in many ways, they are only as serious as we make them. Every marriage will have problems. Let's discuss these problems as carefully and as lovingly as possible, and then restore the marriage relationship as soon as possible.

CHAPTER IX

Three-Way Communication

"He that hath knowledge spareth his words: and a man of understanding is of an excellent spirit." *(Proverbs 17:27)*

Have you ever met an extremely talkative wife who was married to an extremely shy and withdrawn man, or vice versa? The talkative spouse probably would say that she and her husband have good communication. However, she is probably wrong! Real communication does not only include talking. Communication is three-fold. One has not communicated until he talks, listens, and understands. To talk is to express one's thoughts, to listen is to give heed, and to understand is to discern another's thoughts. Someone has said that listening is not only hearing words but receiving what the other person means and feels. To be shut off, not to be heard, is to be rejected. Inattentive listening is one of the main causes of poor communication. The following eight points are some other causes of poor communication.

Communication Barriers

1. Betrayal of confidence. A man does not like to be talked about. He may enjoy hearing his wife tell her best friend, "My husband is the most wonderful man in the world," but he does not like to have his conversations and feelings repeated to others. If a wife reveals her husband's

feelings, she will quickly kill the communication in her marriage.

2. Endless chatter. Women are known to chatter endlessly. If you do not believe this, join a women's gathering sometime. You will notice that, oftentimes, all the woman are talking at once and no one is listening. I noticed that I was more prone to endless chatter when I was at home with babies and young children. I found myself babbling to my husband and to others about things that interested only me.

3. Varied interests. This is one of the biggest destroyers of good communication. When a husband and wife first get married, they have one primary interest—each other. As the marriage years pass, she generally finds her greatest interest in her home and children, while he finds his greatest interest in his job or ministry.

A wise wife will bring herself into her husband's world at least enough to enjoy conversing intelligently about his interests. She also will bring him into her world. Their exchange will improve the communication between them. To ask my husband's opinion about all my decorating changes is just one way I bring him into my world so we can enjoy good conversation.

4. Guilt. When you keep secrets from each other, it hinders communication. Whether that secret is an adulterous affair or a charge on the credit card, it will build a wall between you and make communication difficult.

5. Absence of privacy. If your children always surround you, you will not be free to express some of your most important feelings. Lock the door to your bedroom, then talk, talk, talk.

6. Lack of romance. Romance and commitment encourage a couple's ability to reveal their feelings and risk

humiliation as they express their thoughts to each other. I have always had the ability to speak candidly to my husband about personal and spiritual things. When I share with him in this way, he opens up and shares with me also. Some of our most precious times have come from these moments. When there is no romance or no commitment, it is hard to express thoughts candidly.

7. Different thinking. A man likes to think about one thing at a time, while a woman can carry on several different conversations at one time. However, learn to stay on one train of thought when talking with your husband so your communication can be meaningful.

8. Unresolved conflict. This is a destroyer of our feelings of love for one another and of our communication. Some people like to avoid controversy at any cost. This type person needs to avoid withdrawing from problems. Rather, he needs to admit to himself when problems exist and do what he can to discuss the problem with his spouse or vice versa.

I dated Jack two-and-a-half years before we married. After that long period of dating, I was sure I understood him quite well. However, that was twelve years ago. I was nineteen, and he was twenty-one. Now, we are both in our early thirties, and we have two children. Our needs have changed as we have matured. In fact, our needs are constantly changing in some ways. It would be sad for me to treat him as if his needs hadn't changed at all in twelve years. That is why communication is important. I must constantly come back to the negotiating table with my husband so I can learn to meet his changing needs.

To adapt to our husbands' changing needs, let us not only understand communication but let us also avoid its barriers.

CHAPTER X

How to Handle Jealousy

". . . Charity envieth not . . ."
(I Corinthians 13:4)

I started to title this chapter, "How to Overcome Jealousy," but changed my mind. Perhaps a certain amount of jealousy is healthy. The Bible even tells us that *". . . for I the Lord thy God am a jealous God . . ."* (Exodus 20:5) It is flattering to a husband or a wife to think that a spouse is jealous. Jealousy also can be a built-in safeguard, giving us discernment to see when a relationship between our husbands and the opposite sex is "not quite right."

For these reasons, I changed my chapter title to, "How to Handle Jealousy." If jealousy is incorrectly handled, it can become the dreaded green-eyed monster that destroys our own lives and the lives of those around us. Let me share some ways to handle jealousy.

1. Trust in the Lord. I know this statement sounds like a trite answer to a sometimes overwhelming problem, but faith is the key. *"Above all, taking the shield of faith, wherewith ye shall be able to quench all the fiery darts of the wicked."* (Ephesians 6:16)

I have struggled with jealousy in my life because I am more possessive in nature than some women are. I'm sure the devil is aware of this weak spot in my life, so he sends his fiery darts of jealousy my way trying to destroy me in an area where I am already vulnerable.

I have discovered many practical things I can do to handle this jealousy, but the truth is, there is really only one cure. Seek the Lord and trust Him to preserve the fidelity and purity of our marriage relationship. We also must believe that He will do what we have asked Him to do. If we harbor guilt in our lives, we will have an especially difficult time believing God will answer our prayer. Therefore, it is important to ask forgiveness for our sins and become the person we should be so that we might feel confident of our prayer life. *"And whatsoever we ask, we receive of him, because we keep his commandments, and do those things that are pleasing in his sight."* (I John 3:22)

2. Believe in your desirability as a wife. I think it is difficult for any woman to always understand how her husband can love her and only her for the rest of his life. This is especially hard for one who is more insecure and possessive in nature. A woman who struggles with jealousy may simply need to learn to believe in herself a little more. I believe Chapter 4, "The Root of the Problem," which deals with self-acceptance can help a woman along this line. I also believe that putting into practice the principles of being the right kind of challenge as discussed in the chapter on romance would be a tremendous help to one struggling with self-confidence.

I pray every day for the Lord to give me Christ's confidence. I do not need more confidence in myself and neither does anyone else need confidence in himself. What we do need is a greater sense of whom we can become and what we can do through dependence on Christ.

One of the best ways to develop the right kind of confidence is to avoid comparing ourselves with other women. We should simply be the best God made us to be while seeking most of all to please Christ.

3. Believe in your marriage relationship. We listen to gossip about illicit affairs, talk about it over the telephone for an hour, then get off and mull it over in our minds for the rest of the day. We then wonder why we have no confidence in our marriage.

Philippians 4:8 tells us to think only about things that are positive in nature: *"Finally, brethren, whatsoever things are true, whatsoever things are honest, whatsoever things are just, whatsoever things are pure, whatsoever things are lovely, whatsoever things are of good report; if there be any virtue, and if there be any praise, think on these things."* Don't waste time thinking or fretting about the over-50-percent divorce rate in this country. Rather, spend the time rejoicing about the beautiful Bible plan of marriage that God Himself instituted, and believe in His ability to bless our own marriages as we obey His plan.

4. Emphasize your commitment. A young girl who is going steady will challenge her boyfriend by saying, "I think I want to break up and date around." She usually does not mean a word of it. This conduct is simply her way of handling jealousy, and a poor way indeed.

When a wife says, "If you don't make me feel more secure, I will leave and go home to mother," she is handling her jealousy in a very unwise fashion. Although contrary to the world's position, it is my belief that commitment breeds commitment.

When we were dating, my husband demonstrated repeatedly that he was already very committed to me. I was not that committed at the beginning, but it was his commitment that won me over. He taught me from the very beginning of our relationship the seriousness of our commitment. This did not make me want to take advantage of him. Rather, it encouraged me to do all I could to prove and practice my loyalty to him.

5. Use positive reinforcement. Remember that it was stated previously in this book that praise is one of the keys to completing a spouse. When you praise your husband by saying such things as, "I know many other women would like to have a husband as handsome and stable as you are. I certainly do appreciate the fact that you are loyal to me," you encourage him to be even more faithful.

Let's face it! It is very possible for a man to be faithful to one woman for his entire life, but it isn't easy, especially in this generation. To keep himself pure in today's society, a man needs to feel appreciated for the things he does. Even if you don't have a jealous bone in your body, express from time to time your knowledge of the qualities your husband has that would be appreciated by other women. Also express gratitude for his faithfulness. This type of positive reinforcement will do a lot more to make him want to practice fidelity than scolding or nagging will.

6. Maintain a strong physical relationship. The physical relationship between husband and wife is wonderful in that it is a double safeguard in handling jealousy. It causes a wife to feel more secure in her relationship with her husband, and it also lessens the feelings of temptation that come to both. It is much more unlikely that a person will be tempted to behave immorally when that person is already satisfied with his relationship at home.

7. Set up principles with your husband regarding behavior with the opposite sex. This would be a good thing for engaged couples to do before they are married. My

husband and I set up guidelines for our behavior with the opposite sex very early in our relationship, and that has been a tremendous help to us, especially as the years have passed and we have had more serious problems to deal with in our counseling. Many of these guidelines are included in this book in the next chapter which deals with practicing faithfulness.

8. Don't get too close to the women with whom your husband works. I believe it is a natural instinct for a wife to want to get close to the women with whom her husband works as a way of handling her jealousy. Perhaps she feels that if this woman is her friend, there will be no danger of something improper happening between her husband and his co-worker. However, just the opposite is true. I have been told by several counselors, and have learned by my own counseling experience, that affairs usually happen between a husband and his wife's close friend.

Why does this relationship develop? One reason is that a woman usually lets down her guard around her best friends or closest relatives. Because she trusts her best friend, she may allow guidelines to be broken which have been set by herself and her husband. She also may become careless about what she tells her best friend. She may begin to feel free to discuss with that best friend personal conversations or activities. It is also certain that a best friend will see the weaknesses of a wife and may be tempted, as a husband's co-worker, to fill in where the wife is weak.

For these and several other reasons, it is unwise for a wife to become close friends to the people with whom her husband works or counsels. I do think that there can be some kind of relationship. In fact, for a wife to have a casual friendship with his co-workers is healthy. However, I would not make one of my husband's co-workers a best friend or a confidante.

9. Be thoughtful of the women with whom your husband works. When we do nice things for people, we can become very close to them without spending much social time with them. When a wife is thoughtful of her husband's female co-workers, it causes the wife to feel a part of the relationship between her husband and his co-workers. I feel it causes a healthy three-way relationship.

As I said at the beginning of this chapter, I believe that jealousy can be a good thing. In my travels to different churches, I have occasionally seen some potentially dangerous situations between a pastor and some woman. I have sometimes wished that certain wives would wake up and be a little bit jealous. Proper jealousy can cause a wife to be the best she can be and to appreciate what she has in her husband. Obsessive jealousy, however, is one of those fiery darts from the devil which he sends to us when we are particularly weak.

Let's seek the Lord so we might handle our jealousy properly and have a pure and faithful marriage relationship.

CHAPTER XI

Practicing Faithfulness in Marriage

". . . let every man have his own wife,
and let every woman have her own husband."
(I Corinthians 7:2)

The reason I titled this chapter "Practicing Faithfulness in Marriage" is because I believe that faithfulness is just that—a practice. One reason couples get into trouble and become unfaithful to their marriage vows is because they believe that faithfulness is a state of being. In other words, they believe that a person is either faithful or he is not.

It is my opinion that there lies within each person's heart both a nature to be unfaithful and impure and a nature to do that which is right. Because of this nature, each human being must **practice** faithfulness. Fidelity is not a state of being; fidelity is a planned and rehearsed action.

Since our society no longer tells us that we must remain married to our spouse, it is more important than ever before that a Christian wife practice faithfulness. Humanly speaking, we no longer have anyone telling us what our marriage must be either legally or morally.

The Bible's admonition in Matthew 19:6b and Mark 10:9 remains the same: *"What therefore God hath joined together, let not man put asunder."* Mark 10:11-12 goes on to say, *"And he saith unto them, Whosoever shall put away his wife, and marry another, committeth adultery against her. And if a woman shall put away her husband, and be married to another, she committeth adultery."* The Bible is full of warnings against adultery and divorce. This admonition is definitely reason enough for a Christian wife to plan and practice her behavior with the opposite sex.

How to Practice Faithfulness

1. Don't assume tragedy couldn't happen to you. Some couples never plan to prevent infidelity for themselves or their spouses. Because both came from happy homes, they do not believe their home could be anything less than happy. This type person must realize that the devil sends temptation to **every** person's life, especially if one is a fruitful Christian. Perhaps every Christian will not feel tempted to commit adultery, but every Christian will be strongly tempted to do wrong at some point in his life. The devil sometimes attacks a person in an area where he is weak. However, he sometimes attacks a person in an area where he is particularly strong. Our response to this temptation will depend largely upon the safeguards we have previously established in our lives.

2. Sow what you want to reap. This is especially good advice for a single young lady who is tempted to become too friendly with a married man whose attention she enjoys. To a single young lady, this type of behavior can seem fun and harmless, but it may cause temptation for the married man. The single girl may not take this flirtation seriously, feeling she has nothing to lose. This married man has a lot to lose, including a wife and children. **Therefore, the most important thing to remember is that the single lady has just as much to lose.** The Bible says in Galatians 6:7, *"Be not deceived; God is not mocked: for whatsoever*

a man soweth, that shall he also reap."

You will reap exactly what you have sown. If you sow corn, you will reap corn. If you sow oats, you will reap oats. If a single girl sows temptation, she will reap that same kind of temptation. I tell the girls in my Christian Wife class to treat other women's husbands like they want theirs to be treated, because that is exactly what is going to happen. If you have not been trustworthy in your behavior as a single girl, it will someday be difficult to trust your husband.

3. Be pure in your thoughts and speech. A very wise young preacher once admonished in Hyles-Anderson College chapel to "not even think about what it would have been like if you had married so-and-so." Fantasies about previous boyfriends may seem harmless before temptation comes. Still, when temptation comes, it will not be easy to say, "No!" to the tempter if you have developed a habit of thinking impure thoughts.

Proverbs 17:20 says, *"He that hath a froward heart findeth no good: and he that hath a perverse tongue falleth into mischief."* Is it possible for a person to tell dirty jokes and still live like a good Christian? Perhaps it is, but it is unlikely that the person who tells dirty jokes will be strong enough to live like a good Christian during seasons of great temptation.

4. Be careful about the friends you choose. Because I want to be faithful and committed to my marriage vows, I do not socialize with people whose behavior or speech violates the principles I have set for myself, despite how spiritual that person may seem otherwise. This is good advice for any Christian wife.

5. Avoid outside influences that promote behavior which is contradictory to your principles for fidelity.

Romance novels are lustful and unspiritual. I believe that even Christian romance novels are a waste of time for a married lady. Let's work on our own marriages instead of fantasizing about somebody else's. Rock music promotes everything that is contradictory to the principles of the Christian home. To fill your mind with such music is to set yourself up to fall when temptation strikes. Most television programming promotes sex outside of marriage. I would say that 95 percent of television is dangerous to a committed marriage relationship.   Gossip is not only damaging to those who are being discussed; it is most damaging to your own standard of behavior and to your own security. The best way to respond to gossip is not to listen to it.

   6. Don't compare your husband to other men. It is disloyal to wish your husband was like someone else. It is loyal to accept him as God made him.   He may have weaknesses, but remember that you have weaknesses, too.

   7. Set up principles for behavior with the opposite sex. My husband and I set up some principles for our behavior with the opposite sex before we were married. Let me share a few of them with you.

   • We do not counsel members of the opposite sex on a regular basis.
   • We do not counsel members of the opposite sex in a building alone or late at night.
   • We do not counsel members of the opposite sex about sexual problems. If a lady comes to my husband about a sexual problem, he refers her to me or to some other Christian lady.
   • We do not ride alone in a car with a member of the opposite sex. I have a principle that I will never be the only lady in a car full of men unless one of

those men is my husband.

• We do not participate in suggestive conversation even in jest.

• We do not touch members of the opposite sex other than our families except in the case of a handshake, help off a high step, or general common courtesies. Even in these situations, ladies need to be cautious about men who are overly courteous.

• We do not send gifts or notes of praise to a member of the opposite sex on a regular basis or without including our spouse's name on the note or card. When writing a letter of appreciation to a member of the opposite sex, we also mention that person's spouse.

• We do not allow a member of the opposite sex to become "like a member of the family." We will not allow ourselves to become too dependent on any member of the opposite sex.

• We will not give too much knowledge about ourselves to any member of the opposite sex. We will not discuss personal details about our own life or someone's else's with that person.

8. Establish a "gracious reserve" between you and other members of the opposite sex. For years I have watched my mother, Mrs. Beverly Hyles, maintain what I call a "gracious reserve" between herself and members of the opposite sex. Her ability to be gracious and friendly yet never indiscreet in any way has often amazed me, especially because she has always been so beautiful. It is not unusual for my mother to receive some compliment from a stranger as we are out in public. This attention is quite an "egobuster" for my sisters and me.

In the last few years, I have tried to observe just

what it is that causes a woman to have a "gracious reserve." What is the difference between the behavior of a woman like my mother and a woman whom other ladies "just don't trust"? The difference can be described in two words—body language.

Proverbs has a lot to say about body language. Proverbs 6:12-13 says, *"A naughty, a wicked man walketh with a froward mouth. He winketh with his eyes, he speaketh with his feet, he teacheth with his fingers."* Through body language, we can learn so much about a person's character. Here are some ideas about having proper body language.

Be Pure

• Look a man only in the eyes. Not only should you look a man in the eyes, but you should keep a discreet look in your eye. I cannot describe exactly what a look of discretion is, but I have seen what it is not. Maybe being aware of how we are coming across will help us look at a man properly.

• Maintain a safe distance between yourself and a man when you are talking with him. A safe distance will keep a short girl from looking up at a taller man like she has just been struck by lightning. You need to stand far enough away from a man so that you are able to look at him in a manner that is not flirtatious.

• Stand in an appropriate posture when talking to a member of the opposite sex. A slouching posture can look flirtatious when it is not. I try to stand straight and show my respect for the person to whom I am talking.

• Do not use inappropriate body movements when communicating with others. There may be something cute about talking with your hands or having expressive eyes. Still, I have seen some very indiscreet girls, when talking with others, use muscles I did not know existed. Remember, body language reveals a lot about a person's character.

• Speak to a man in a courteous, but formal, voice. We should remember to be gracious to other men and not make them feel uncomfortable. On the other hand, there should be a definite difference in the tone of voice a wife uses with her husband and the one she uses with other men.

• Never follow a man with your eyes after he has passed you. I have seen some young girls get so excited about passing a married man whom they admired that they practically fell apart emotionally. Surely a lady can learn to make a man feel welcome and respected without causing him (or his wife) to have a cardiac arrest.

• When speaking to a couple, always greet the wife first and include her in the conversation as much as possible.

• Never compliment a man about his appearance. One may tell a good male friend in the presence of his wife that she likes his tie. That would be very different from saying, "Wow! You sure look nice today."

My college president, Dr. Wendell Evans, is a man whom my husband and I admire tremendously. While I was a student at Hyles-Anderson College, Dr. Evans admonished the entire student body often by saying, "I would rather be a prude than a casualty." Proverbs 27:12 says something similar: *"A prudent man foreseeth the evil, and hideth himself; but the simple pass on, and are punished."* A simple or foolish man will walk into temptation's trap and will suffer the consequences. However, a prudent man will go the extra mile to prevent the trouble which might be lurking just ahead. Let's save ourselves, our husbands, our children, and others the pain of adultery and divorce by being prudish and faithful in our actions.

Let's establish a "gracious reserve" that will show others that we, within and without, are truly beautiful ladies.

CHAPTER XII

Loving Your In-laws

"And Ruth said, Intreat me not to leave thee, or to return from following after thee: for whither thou goest, I will go; and where thou lodgest, I will lodge: thy people shall be my people, and thy God my God." (Ruth 1:16)

When I was first married, I wanted so badly for my in-laws to be pleased with me as their son's wife. Jack and I had dated for two-and-a-half years before we were married, and we had nothing but good memories of our time spent as a couple with our parents to that point. I therefore expected when my in-laws saw my "perfection" as a wife that it would only enhance my relationship with them. (As inexperienced as I was in some areas, I am not sure how I expected to be so perfect.)

What I did not realize was that while I was fantasizing about my perfection, something very difficult was taking place in the hearts and minds of his mother and father as well as in the minds of my own parents. I regret that it was not until I had my own son that I began to realize just what took place during that time.

My husband and I are both the youngest in our immediate families. When we got married, a major stage of our parents' lives ended. Though there was a lot of life yet to be lived for them and they have accomplished much since then, I am sure they felt unneeded and somewhat

useless as they adjusted to the "empty nest." I have very
few regrets in my life, but if I had my life to live over, I
would change the way I treated my in-laws those first few
years of my married life. The following are some things that
I would change:

1. I would not try to impress my in-laws. Most new
brides want to impress their new in-laws when they first
have them over for dinner. There are many reasons why
this is not a good idea. One is because there are too many
possibilities of things going wrong. The main reason is that
the **last** type of person a mother-in-law feeling unneeded
should be around is someone who is "perfect."

Human beings do not enjoy being around someone
who seems perfect, yet most human beings try to appear
perfect before others. That is an amusing thing about
human nature to me. I am not saying that we should put
our worst foot forward, but people will feel closer to us if
we are willing to reveal some weakness.

During those first few years of marriage, my in-law's
visits were major events. I had to clean the house until it
was spotless. I felt that I must prepare at least a seven-
course meal and serve it on the china. I was actually trying
to "put on" in a way that I was not really experienced
enough to do as nineteen-year-old bride. I was too proud
to ask for help, and so I "put on" until I was exhausted.

Obviously, I did not look forward to their visits, and
the fault was my own. If I had it to do all over, I hope I
would realize the selfishness of my motives at a very difficult
time in my in-law's lives. I hope that I would serve them
and enjoy them without trying to impress them.

2. I would ask for their advice. My mom and dad
prepared me in many ways to be a good wife. I owe a great
debt to them for that preparation. Nevertheless, there are

many things a wife and homemaker can learn only by experience in her own home. I doubt if there has ever been a woman who was an expert homemaker the first year she was married. Still, few women are willing to go to their in-laws for advice. A woman will call her own mother for advice, but she usually resents the suggestions of a mother-in-law. Why? Because her motive in being a good daughter-in-law is not to meet the needs of her in-laws, but rather to impress them.

When someone is feeling unneeded and useless, what can meet her needs better than a daughter-in-law who is less experienced in her mother-in-law's field? If I had it to do over, I would call my mother-in-law and ask for her recipes, her suggestions on housekeeping, and other wifely and motherly advice.

3. I would not be offended when they offered suggestions. I would realize that my in-laws had much to offer my husband and me. I would realize that suggestions by in-laws are simply their way of finding a niche, a place where they fit in this new relationship with their son and his new wife.

4. I would tell them how important they are to my husband. It is common for a mother-in-law to spend time talking about the things she has done for her son. Many times, new brides resent this. They feel that the mother-in-law is simply trying to devalue her son's new marriage relationship. This is not true at all. The mother-in-law just desperately needs to feel she still has some kind of identity with the child who has just left her home. The wise new wife will be forbearing and will not only agree with her mother-in-law's comments, but will beat her to the punch by making some loving comments of her own.

5. I would encourage them to spend time alone

with my husband. Every son-in-law or daughter-in-law sometimes gets the feeling that he or she is a fifth wheel—someone who does not fit in with the activities or the conversations of the spouse's immediate family. When we feel left out, human nature tells us to try to dominate the conversation or to withdraw and pout. Scriptural principles, however, tell us that we should think of others and not ourselves. *"Be kindly affectioned one to another with brotherly love; in honour preferring one another."* (Romans 12:10) As our in-laws try to establish a new relationship with their offspring, we should encourage them to spend some time alone with him. On the humorous side, this will spare us the boredom of listening to stories which do not involve or interest us. Of course, there also should be a time when a wife "jumps in" and includes herself in the activities and conversations of her new family. She will learn that there really are some interesting things to be learned about her new husband's past.

6. I would do something when my in-laws visit that says, "I'm glad you came!" I do not "put on" for my in-laws. They prefer eating at restaurants to a home-cooked meal. Because of their preference, I usually do not cook dinner when they come to visit. Sometimes I do. Recently, when my in-laws came for a visit, I not only cooked a special meal the first night they were in my home, I also decorated the dining room and gave a birthday party for my mother-in-law. I do not always do things like that, but I always try to have something prepared that says, "I'm glad you came!" This special welcome may be a batch of cookies, a small gift, or something you know your in-laws like.

7. I would be thoughtful at birthdays. Every young bride should get a list from her husband of his family's

birthdays and mark them on her calendar, then make an effort to send at least a card to every family member on his special day. Being thoughtful of people on special occasions is one way to feel close to them even if you are unable to spend much time with them.

What We Did Right

I feel I made some mistakes when I first became a daughter-in-law. There are many things I learned to do differently the hard way. However, there are some decisions my husband and I made about in-laws when we first married that have helped our marriage tremendously. They are as follows:

• We always stood with each other. My husband gave my in-laws and me every indication that I was first in his life, even when I was perhaps being unreasonable. With my parents' advice, I also did all I could to be sure my husband knew he was number one with me. Every young couple should decide that they will always stand with each other when in conflict with their in-laws, even if they think their spouse is wrong.

• We did not defend our parents to each other. I'm sure there have been times when one of us did not agree with the other's parents. I'm also sure that, many of those times, our opinions have been wrong. We have not defended them to each other at these times. Rather, we have stood true to our commitment to put each other first, and it has paid off in our relationship.

• We shared very little of our personal life with our in-laws and made every effort to speak positively about each other to our parents. My husband and I often counsel couples whose marriages we feel could have been saved much heartache if the in-laws had not become involved with their children's problems. It is easy to overlook the faults of one's child. It is much more difficult to overlook the faults of that child's spouse, especially when one's child is affected negatively. The wise wife will be very careful about speaking negatively about her husband to her parents. On the other hand, a wife also should be careful about speaking negatively to her husband about his family.

I have learned, and am still learning, how to have an unselfish love relationship with my in-laws. It is not difficult because of the great people they are. They have truly been good examples of what parents should be. I enjoy their company not only as my in-laws, but as my very good friends.

When we were first married, my in-laws would call and dutifully talk to me for awhile, then excitedly ask to talk to my husband. A few years ago, they called and talked to him for awhile, then excitedly asked if they could talk to me! When we finished talking and I hung up the phone, my husband said, "I think they like talking to you more than they like talking to me." I realized then that I had learned how to be what I should be to my in-laws.

Now that we have children, my in-laws talk dutifully on the phone to Jack and me and then excitedly ask to talk to Jaclynn and Kenny. I don't think I am their favorite anymore, but I love them anyway!

Let us unselfishly love our in-laws.

CHAPTER XIII

Happily Married With Children

"Lo, children are an heritage of the Lord . . .
Happy is the man that hath his quiver full of
them." (Psalm 127:3-5)

There is a popular book written on the subject of
marriage entitled, *How To Be Happy Though Married.* I
have always found this title rather humorous. Those of us
who view the world with some bit of sarcasm could
interpret that title to mean that happiness is quite difficult
to grasp for those who are in the miserable state of
marriage.

I, for one, found happiness to be quite attainable
when I became married, even from the early days of
adjustment. Actually, I found marriage to be very little
adjustment at all. However, the early days of parenthood
were quite a different story.

I had longed to be a mother and was very excited
when our daughter Jaclynn was born ten years ago. I read
all the parenting books I could get my hands on, and felt
rather prepared for the whole experience. Still, I had no
idea what an adjustment having children could be in a life
and a marriage. It is especially hard to have a happy
marriage and to have young children at the same time, yet
a good marital relationship is the best gift a parent can give
to her child. In fact, the best way to teach those young
children many things about life and relationships is for a
wife to love her spouse. Because of this adjustment, I

would like to give some hints about how to have a good marriage all the way from pregnancy through child rearing.

Helpful Hints

1. Try to wait some time before having your first baby. Some women begin to long for a baby shortly after the wedding is over. It is as though women always need to be conquering new territory. Once the husband has become "conquered territory," women think it is time to move on to something else. The opposite is true. Marriage is to be enjoyed as top priority in a woman's life for as long as she and her husband live. Therefore, a wife should take time to enjoy those first days of being a wife, because she will only be alone with her husband as a new bride for a short time. She should allow herself to adjust and to enjoy this quickly passing stage of life. I recommend to the students in my Christian Wife class that they wait until they have been married at least one or two years before they have children.

2. When you are expecting a baby, determine to remain physically attractive. I do not believe pregnancy should be a time when a woman gains all the weight she wants to. Obviously, some weight should be gained to produce a healthy baby. My doctor told me that twenty-five pounds is a good, average weight gain. However, pregnancy is not the time to throw caution to the wind as far as eating habits and appearance are concerned. I recommend eating a normal amount of food while cutting back drastically on "junk food."

Our society today caters more than ever to the pregnant lady. Maternity clothes are more fashionable than ever. A woman has no excuse not to look her best. The months of pregnancy are an important time to take especially good care of one's hair, complexion, and physical hygiene.

3. Determine to be romantically attractive during pregnancy. If a lady is careful about what she eats, there is no reason why she cannot feel and look attractive to her husband in a feminine nightgown. I have done enough marriage counseling to realize how important it is that a wife stay romantically attractive and attentive during pregnancy. Most doctors will now tell you that it is perfectly all right to keep a normal intimate relationship during and after pregnancy. Some doctors, especially in past years, have suggested abstinence during the six-week period after pregnancy. I have counseled with women whose marriages have been permanently damaged and almost destroyed because of their decision to put their romance on hold for awhile after childbirth. I realize that a husband has a responsibility to be patient and self-controlled during this time, but a wife also has a responsibility to remember her priorities.

4. During pregnancy, determine to keep interests other than the pregnancy. I stated earlier in a chapter on communication that when a husband and wife first get married, they both have one primary interest—each other. As the marriage matures, a husband's primary interest becomes a job or a ministry. A wife's primary interest becomes her home and children. A lot of this change begins to take place when a wife finds out that she is expecting her first child. How she handles this change may determine how close she and her husband will be for the rest of their marriage.

When a woman comes home from the doctor's office and announces that she is expecting a baby, her husband is terribly excited. He pampers her and refuses to allow her to pick up anything heavy—for a few weeks. After a few weeks, he settles down and returns to the normal routine of living. Men generally do not get as excited about things they cannot see as women do. A woman can get excited about things that she alone feels. During the first few months of pregnancy, she can feel many changes taking place while her husband doesn't see anything happening at all. If she is not careful, she will begin to eat, drink and sleep while thinking of nothing but the coming baby, and she will drift apart from her husband.

The wise Christian wife will set aside time to enjoy every stage of her pregnancy. However, she also should set aside time to enjoy her husband's interests. What she should do during her entire pregnancy is find a way to bring him into her world and to find a way to keep entering his.

Share Your World

A. Ask him to accompany you to the doctor to hear the baby's heartbeat or to see the ultrasound. While a man may not get excited about what he cannot see, he will oftentimes be much more excited than the wife about what he **can** see and hear. When he is unable to attend the doctor's appointment, give him as much information as you can when you talk with him again.

B. Take childbirth classes together. My husband dreaded the whole idea of childbirth classes. However, after experiencing just one class, he was much more excited than I was. My husband and I were blessed to have a Christian lady come into our home and give childbirth instruction. While I strongly believe in childbirth classes, I also realize that some classes do not have an atmosphere which is appropriate for Christians.

C. Include him in decision-making while expecting. Get his input as you decorate the nursery, choose a name, and so forth.

D. If it is permissible, visit his place of ministry or employment a little more than usual.

E. Go soul winning together or visit your husband's Sunday school class with him.

F. Make an extra special effort to remain interested and knowledgeable about his favorite sport or hobby.

5. Before the baby is born, discuss with your husband what differences you expect to take place and how you hope to react to them.

6. Put the baby on a schedule. I am a firm believer in putting a baby on a schedule. When I was expecting my first child, I read a book entitled, *My First 300 Babies* by Gladys West Hendrick. I highly recommend this book for every new mother. I realize that babies cannot be scheduled in the same way as adults, and to people who have never scheduled a baby, the idea seems ridiculous and impossible.

I must say that to schedule a baby takes hard work and some time, but the reward is not that long in coming. The reward that I experienced was the ability to predict how much I was going to accomplish on any given day while thoroughly enjoying my baby and my other relationships. I believe that a schedule is especially important if a mother is nursing her baby. A husband and wife can feel a lot of frustration during the months of nursing unless some type of schedule is established.

7. Include him in caring for the baby. I think it is unwise for a wife to tease about her husband's inability to

change a diaper, to give a bath, etc. I felt that, in some ways, my husband was better at handling our children than I was, and I told him so. This type of praise encouraged him to take part in the process of caring for our babies. Of course, I was the primary care giver to our children, but his involvement gave us just another opportunity to have things in common. Tell him specifically the ways he benefits the children.

8. Schedule time to be thoughtful of your husband. If a woman does not schedule time for her husband, she neglects one of the most important people in her life. This is especially true during the days of caring for small children. A woman should schedule time to bake a treat, write a note, buy a card, or give a back rub. She should schedule time to prove to her husband that he is number one in their home.

9. Determine to stay in church. I believe that the Lord will bless a mother who does her best to be in church. After a baby is born can be the easiest time to backslide. I have always felt especially close to my husband while sitting by his side during the church services. I decided before our first child was born that I would still be by his side during church **after** the birth of our baby as much as possible.

I do not believe a baby should be taken to church with a high fever. My babies were cared for in the nursery of the largest church in the world, and, in spite of all the germs to which they have been exposed, they have been very healthy children. They did go through a sick stage during their first year, as so many babies do. However, we were in church as much as possible, and I believe the Lord has blessed us for it.

10. Use baby-sitters. The mother who says, "I have never left my children," is probably not a very good wife.

Lest you misunderstand, let me say that I do not approve of children being left with one baby-sitter after another. During my children's first year of life, I left them with a baby-sitter for basically two reasons: (1) to go soul winning and (2) to go on a weekly date with my husband. I decided that these were priorities, so I did not feel guilty about leaving our children. I did leave them with the same baby-sitter each time so they would be secure and unafraid.

11. Never disagree on discipline in front of the children. It is very harmful to a child and to a marriage for a wife to undermine her husband's disciplinary actions. Even if he may be wrong, a wife should defend her husband's discipline. She should refer the children's questions to her husband when he is at home so it is clear to the children that daddy is the leader. Usually, I believe it is better for a child to be punished unjustly than for a child to see an example of a disobedient wife. (Of course, that would not apply to child abuse in a home.)

12. Let your children see you express some appropriate affection. It is my belief that it is good for a child to see some hugging and kissing between mom and dad. Of course, most other types of marital affection would be completely inappropriate. When hugging and kissing openly become taboo, it puts unnecessary strain on the romance in a marriage.

13. Teach your children to respect your privacy. One of the biggest secrets to being happily married even though you have children is to have a secure lock on your bedroom door and to use it!

14. Show your excitement when daddy comes home. What makes for a joyful marriage in a house whose walls ring with the noise of children? Having a leader (Daddy) who is spoiled by his family brings joy to daddy,

but this especially brings joy to mother and the children. Remember, however, that small children learn very little through verbal instruction. Most of what they learn is learned from example. That means children will not spoil daddy and greet him with enthusiasm unless they see that mother does.

15. Look at the future. I was startled to learn through my reading in recent years that the average husband and wife will live alone together for thirty years after their children have grown and left the nest. The marriage relationship is really our most permanent relationship. It would be silly for us not to invest the best of ourselves in it.

Most mothers read and study for hours trying to discover how to do a good job of rearing their children. When those children disappoint her, the average mother will invest much time deciding how she, the mother, can improve. When her husband disappoints her, she assumes he is the problem and gives very little thought to the solution.

Put quite simply, I'm afraid that most mothers love their children more than they love their husbands. To love our children more than we love our husbands is to harm **both our husbands and our children**. It also disappoints Christ Whose plan was for a woman to put hubby number one. Most of all, it hurts the wife, who is investing very little time into her most permanent relationship.

Let's keep hubby number one!

CHAPTER XIV

Financial Bliss
by Earlyne Stephens

"Seest thou a man diligent in his business? he shall stand before kings." (Proverbs 22:29)

A study has been made showing that financial problems is one of the four greatest causes of divorce. If this is true, one must make a study of his own personal finances to see if he has the proper understanding of handling his money. It has been said that financial problems have destroyed more marriages than almost any other thing. I once heard a man who was deeply in debt say, "I have one wife, eight credit cards, and two check books which, all together, got me into financial trouble."

Don't "Keep Up With the Joneses"

The first word I want us to consider is *contentment.* If you are contented, you will be happy. A happy person is a contented person. To be contented means to be satisfied with what we have. The Bible says in Philippians 4:11, *"Not that I speak in respect of want, for I have learned, in whatsoever state I am, therewith to be content."*

One morning at Hyles-Anderson College I met one of the gentlemen teachers who said, "Hello, Mrs. Stephens, how are you today?"

I said, "Fine, thank you. How are you?"

He replied, "Just right."

I stopped and thought, "That is a wonderful answer which praises Jesus. He is just right. He is satisfied with everything in his life. He has probably thanked God already this morning for everything in his life because he thinks that everything is 'just right.' "

That was a lesson for me that morning. I want to think that everything in my life is "just right." The Bible says, *"In everything give thanks."* That means we must be contented and, if we are contented, we will say like the gentleman I met that everything is "just right" in our lives.

I read a little saying the other day that said, "There is a new disease in America today. It is, 'I saw it and I want it.' " That is the way with many of us. We see things, and we think we must have them.

My brother and my preacher, Dr. Jack Hyles taught a few years ago on the subject, "Acquisition Does Not Satisfy the Appetite." He said that if we get a new home, we **must** have new furniture for that new home. Our old furniture looks terrible. It just doesn't fit in our new home. We therefore purchase new furniture, and we are so proud of our new home and new furniture. We then look around and see that we **must** have new carpeting for the floors. It gives such warmth to the new home. We have the carpet laid, and we look around and see that our old drapes just do not match that new carpeting. They look awful, so we must have new drapes. After we get new drapes, we notice our next door neighbor's backyard fence. We had not even thought about having a new fence. If the neighbor has one, we **must** have one, too. After all, we cannot be the only one in the neighborhood without a fence. The cycle of wanting goes on and on. If we can just be content with what we have, we will be happier people, and we will make those around us happier.

We should learn to buy only what we can afford. We do not need to try to "keep up with the Jones." Did you know that the "Joneses" are not happy? They just keep buying all the time and are never satisfied. I think contentment is one of the most important things you can learn when controlling your finances.

Do you know how we can be happy? Just give to other people and try to fill their needs. I sometimes look at some of the ladies I know and think of how far in debt their husbands are. How can their husbands be happy? They will never have anything to give away. We get our happiness from giving, but so often we spend everything our husbands make and rob them of the joy of giving.

We should learn to keep our entertainment simple. We do not need to dress up and go out to eat in the most expensive restaurants to have a good time. Please don't misunderstand me. I think we should go out occasionally. We just don't need to feel as if we must spend money to be happy or to enjoy life.

Someone once asked me what I did to have a good time. I started thinking. I could not remember when I had done anything special to have a good time. I used to dress up and go into Chicago to Orchestra Hall for entertainment, but I haven't done that in many months. Then I started thinking that I have a good time wherever I am. I have a good time at my office. I have a good time at home. I have a good time with my friends. I have a good time in my Sunday school class. I have a good time at church. I have a good time in choir practice. I have a good time wherever I am! I have learned that I can be happy without spending lots of money; therefore, I have learned to be content. If we can just keep our entertainment simple, then we will not have to spend lots of money to be entertained.

Our preacher has also taught us that we should enjoy everything we do three times. We do that by performing these three simple steps.

- anticipate
- participate
- meditate

We should look forward to the activity — anticipate it. We should enjoy it while we are doing it — participate in it. Then we should look back upon it, think about what a good time we had, and enjoy it again — mediate on it. That way, we can enjoy everything we do three times.

Our mother, Coystal Hyles, always enjoyed going out to eat, especially in a restaurant. If my brother and I suggested going out to eat to her, she would be so excited. The first thing she would do in anticipation was go to the telephone, call a friend, and say, "Guess what! We are going out to eat Saturday morning." My, how she would look forward to going, and when Saturday morning came, she would enjoy herself so much. Maybe she would see some people she knew. She just had a wonderful time while she was there. Now, of course you know what she did when she arrived home. She would call a friend and tell her how much fun she had. She enjoyed going out to breakfast three times!

We need to keep our children's tastes simple, too. I am sure there were many things I did while growing up that cost money, but many of those things I cannot recall. Some of the sweetest times we had as a family did not cost anything.

I remember going out with mother and daddy to

pick up pecans. I would have my little tin bucket. My father was a large, strong man, and he would shake the pecan tree. This made many pecans fall, and I would pick up the nuts and fill my tin bucket. That was so much fun!

Look back upon your life and try to remember the things you did with your family that didn't cost anything, yet everyone enjoyed them very much. Did you pick apples, visit the zoo, fish, hike trails, or picnic? Those are things our family remembers, and you can do these things with your children. They can have fun without spending lots of money.

Let's be like the gentleman who, when I asked him how he was, said, "I am just right." I think that gentleman had learned contentment. Let's not "keep up with the Joneses" because **things** are just not going to make us happy.

Let Your Budget Be Your Boss

The second word I want you to consider is the word *budget*. Prepare a budget and let that budget be your boss concerning your finances. When we go on a trip, we plan a schedule for that trip. When we plan to lose weight, we have a diet and schedule our eating. When we start the day, we have a schedule and regulate our day. So why can't we have a budget? A budget is simply scheduling our money and deciding what we are going to do with it.

Do you remember when folks put their extra change in a jar located on the top shelf of the kitchen cabinet? Can you remember your mother doing that? My mother talked about her mother doing the same thing. She would take money from the jar to purchase needed items for the family until the money was gone. When the jar was empty, the spending ended. There was no more money, so there would be no more purchasing. Some people still live like that. As long as the money lasts, they can make purchases. However, when the money is gone, the spending stops. With this method, it is impossible to spend more than you have.

You can also use envelopes in place of the little jar in the kitchen. You can take envelopes and write on the front of each the name of the budget item. When you get paid, put the allotted amount in each envelope as shown on your budget and spend only this amount.

Most people are living on the credit basis. There are no little jars; there are no envelopes. Therefore, there is no limit to our spending. The only way we will have a limit is the limit on the credit card. We simply are bound to the credit company and keep buying until we reach our limit.

Preparing and Keeping a Budget

1. List your expenses. On paper, list your expenses on a monthly basis. Write down the amounts of your fixed expenses such as your tithe, house or rental payment, taxes, insurance, and so forth. Then decide what you can spend on your variable expenses such as food, utilities, clothing, medicine, entertainment, savings, and so forth. You might want to keep a diary for about a month before making up your budget to see exactly how much you currently spend on these items. Just mark down how much you spend on each budget item and you can know what you will need for a month for each item.

2. List your net income on a monthly basis. Your gross income is the amount of money you earn before anything like taxes and insurance has been deducted.

3. Compare your expenses with your income. Hold your breath! Your expenses are **not** to exceed your income. There is no way you can survive if you have more expenses than you have income. If your expenses exceed your income, you must either get more income or reduce your expenses.

4. Decide when you are going to pay your expenses. If you get paid twice each month, divide your expenses between the two pay periods. Now you have assigned every item in the budget to the appropriate payday on which you will pay it. When you receive your paycheck, look at the budget for that pay period and immediately pay all the items you have designated to pay. At the next pay period, you will pay the remaining bills due.

Financial Setbacks

Let me discuss some of the problems you will encounter so you will not get discouraged.

1. Maybe your checkbook will show more money than you really have. I like to use duplicate checks because I always have a record of the checks I have written. If you fail to write down a check you have written, you will have a duplicate, enabling you to keep your records current and correct. To keep your checkbook in good order, always **subtract** the checks written and **add** the amount of the deposits made. You laugh, but how many times have mistakes been made when a person writes a check and mistakenly adds the amount of the check to the balance they have in the bank. Always reconcile your bank statement when you receive it from the bank each month. Make sure that your records are the same as the bank records. I saw a little saying the other day that was so cute.

"How can I be overdrawn? I still have checks left!"

2. Another problem you will encounter is impulsive buying. Learn to make a list of things you need before you go shopping. Purchase the needed items and go home. Try hard not to buy anything on the spur of the moment. Do not ever buy impulsively. Compare prices; sometimes you can find things cheaper elsewhere. There have been times when I felt as if I just **had** to make a purchase. I just could not live without it. When I did not buy it, I was so proud of myself. If I did buy it, I was sorry for having done it. Learn not to buy impulsively.

There are four little statements I have heard almost all my life. They should be asked before making any purchases.

- Do I really need this?
- Do I need something more than I need this?
- Do I have the money to buy this?
- Can I do without this?

3. Another problem you will have is gift giving. So many people now emphasize the gifts and not the giver. Do you know that you can break your husband's budget by just going to showers? When the bride opens a beautiful gift, we each would like to be the one who says, "I gave her that." But you can't always give the most beautiful gift at the expense of your family. You will stay in debt constantly.

Organize your giving. Make a list of birthdays. Plan your Christmas gifts.

Let me tell you about a birthday gift I received some years ago. A friend wanted to get me a present, and she didn't have much money that week. She said she only had $1.50, and do you know what she bought me? She bought me four little fruit juice glasses for $1.19. She said to me, "I hope you enjoy these. I have some just like them, and I really enjoy mine." Each time I drank out of those glasses, I thought about her. It isn't the price of the gift, it is knowing the giver, knowing she loves you, and knowing she did not go into debt buying a present.

One lady who is a nurse gives a baby thermometer at baby showers. She gives blue ones for boys and pink ones for girls. When she is invited to a shower, the mother always knows exactly what she will be getting, and she is thrilled. Find something that isn't too expensive, and when you give it from your heart, you will not want to be the one with the prettiest present.

Many times, if we just use our heads and not as much money, we could be so much happier; the person for whom you are shopping would be happier, too. You don't have to go against your budget to give gifts.

Your Children Can Budget, Too!

When a child is about ten or eleven years old, he could be given a small recipe-size file box containing five small envelopes. The amount of money to be placed in each envelope comes from a planning session with mom and dad. They can get together and decide what the child's expenses for the year will be, divide that amount by twelve, and give the child that amount each month. As the child earns money and receives gifts of money, he can put that money into at least three envelopes and perhaps all five of them. One envelope is for the tithe. One is for clothing. One is for savings. One is for gifts, and the last one is for the child's personal spending.

The "spend" envelope contains money the child can

spend in any way he chooses. The "gift" envelope contains money allocated to buy gifts for occasions such as birthdays or Christmas for friends or family. Teach your children to plan early to earn the money they will spend on gifts for special occasions. The "clothing" envelope contains money to purchase the child's clothing. Of course, the child should be taught that the tithe is **always** the **first** money to be set aside.

Following this procedure will teach children to tithe first and save money from each paycheck. When the money is gone from each envelope, there should be no more money until the next pay period. Children will learn to be responsible to pay for items they need or want, and when the money is gone, there will be no more new clothing, no more gifts, and no more spending. The age to start using this method with your child will depend on the child. Some children could learn this at age eight and some would not be able to learn this until later.

Let's plan our budget and keep that budget as our financial boss.

Be Disciplined

The next word I want to discuss is *discipline.* After making our financial plan or budget, stick to it. Be disciplined and follow the budget. Live by that budget. Learn to say, "No!" to yourself about the things you would like to have or think you want yet know you cannot afford.

Learn to say, "No!" to your children. You do not need to spoil them by getting them everything they want or think they want. A friend of mine once said that we as parents do without **necessities** in order to give our children all their **wants**. There is a lot of wisdom in those words.

Say, "No!" to your children and you will have happier children.

Learn to say, "No!" at the grocery store. I know we women are alike. God made us to serve, and we want to buy everything in the grocery store so we can go home and try new recipes. We must watch our spending in the grocery store. I find that I buy more if I am hungry. So I have found it is better if I eat before going to shop for groceries.

Let's be content, be budgeted, be disciplined, and therefore, make our husbands happy. If you don't have it, don't spend it!

CHAPTER XV

Attitudes that Increase Commitment

"Verily, verily, I say unto you,
Except a corn of wheat fall into the ground
and die, it abideth alone: but if it die, it
bringeth forth much fruit." (John 12:24)

During most of my years of being Mrs. Jack Schaap, I have loved my husband because he was considerate and kind and because he has many attributes I would like to emulate. I now love him for different reasons. Most of my life I have loved my parents, Dr. and Mrs. Hyles, because they were good and kind, and to be honest, being their daughter brought me some popularity and material gain. Through the years, however, I have learned to love these three people because God wanted me to do so. My love turned to commitment. When love turns to commitment, the flowers become more beautiful, the birds sound sweeter and, most of all, my respect for myself improves. I committed myself not to the strengths, but to the weaknesses of "my people." It was the least I could do because they had committed themselves to my weaknesses a long time ago.

I stated earlier that God gives wives an opportunity to show Him that we love Him. That opportunity is called obedience. We can best show God that we love Him by obeying our closest biblical authority. For a wife, that authority is her husband. When we love our husbands because they love and please us, we show God that we love our husbands. If we love our husbands when we have lost our desire to do so, we show God that we love God Himself.

During much of my life, I was considered a spoiled preacher's kid. I road along on the coattails of my parents' fame and spirituality and knew very little of hardships in life. During that time, I must admit that I was like Peter in John 20. I was merely fond of Jesus.

There came a time in my life, however, when I began to love and commit myself to people when times were hard. I did it because it was what God wanted me to do. It was then I realized that I was no longer fond of Jesus; I knew that I deeply loved Him. I do not say this to brag, for my heart is prone to wander. I want and need to learn to love Him more. Yet I am as sure as I can possibly be that I love Jesus with some depth.

Every new bride believes her groom is perfect. She refuses to look at his weaknesses. Sometimes a wife can go for years without ever admitting to herself that her spouse has weaknesses at all. However, there is usually some time in the marriage when she comes face to face with weaknesses she cannot ignore. What she does then determines the outcome of her relationships and the outcome of her life.

I am not talking here about overlooking blatant sin. I do not believe that is helpful to a wife or her husband. I **am** talking about commitment to the **weaknesses** of our loved ones, our husbands in particular. Jack Schaap is committed to the weaknesses of Cindy Schaap, and I am committed to his. I must admit that his weaknesses are much fewer than mine, but I **am** committed to his weaknesses.

The bottom line of a good marriage is commitment. Commitment is a word which, if never used, sounds dull and unattractive. When used repeatedly, though, it becomes all those things you thought you would find in the new and glamorous—and more. Because of this, I would like to share some principles that develop commitment in marriage.

Commit Yourself

1. Expect things to go wrong. John 16:33 says, *"These things I have spoken unto you, that in me ye might have peace. In the world ye shall have tribulation: but be of good cheer; I have overcome the world."* In this passage, God is telling us that tribulations (or problems) are a constant. This is particularly true in a marriage and a family. There will always be daily problems that each spouse must face together. There should be a decision made from the marriage altar that problems will be faced in exactly that way—together.

2. Don't change when things go wrong. My dad, Dr. Jack Hyles, once preached a sermon which I believe was entitled, "Don't Make a Decision When Your Decision Maker Is Broken." The poorest time to decide that a divorce is inevitable is when a couple is enduring or has endured serious marital problems. For example, no one thinks clearly when she has just heard that her spouse has had an adulterous affair. To immediately decide to get a divorce at such a time would be very unwise. Oftentimes, couples make such a decision when they are under extreme pressure only to regret their decision for the rest of their lives.

3. Decide before problems come to whom you will

go for advice. Some couples divorce unnecessarily because some well-meaning relative or peer told them it was the right thing to do. I'm afraid that many wives handle their marriage problems by calling their ten best friends for advice and then following the advice most frequently given or the one piece of advice they want to hear. This is a tragic way to handle life. A wife should have a name in her mind, perhaps of a pastor or a pastor's wife, of someone to whom she would go for advice in a time of marriage crisis. This person should probably not be a family member or a close friend.

4. Don't blame other people for your marital problems. Not only should we not blame **anyone** else for our marital problems, but we should also be quick to blame ourselves. Our marital problems can never be solved until we face the fact that the problem lies within us. When we blame others, we lose our trust in people and become suspicious. This is always a dangerous frame of mind.

5. Decide to cherish the old relationships more than the new. Many marriages are dissolved because one spouse decided that a new romance would be more fun and attractive. As stated earlier, one must **try** commitment first before she discovers how fun and attractive it is. The opposite is true of lack of commitment. Its most attractive days are the first ones. The relationship goes downhill from there.

6. Decide to be patient with God's leading in your marriage. We must realize that God is always working in our lives and He always responds to our prayers about our marriages. Every time we pray, God **does** do something in answer to that prayer. Sometimes things go from bad to worse after we pray for deliverance. Yet, even that can be a sure sign that God is truly at work in our marriage. A

truly committed couple will continue to take their problems to the Lord in prayer and **leave** their problems with Him.

7. Remember the commitment which Christ has shown to us. My husband Jack Schaap has often shared with me and others that one of the foundational principles we must understand in order to grow as Christians is that Jesus loves us just because He loves us. That is to say that He does not love us any more because we look nice or behave well. Neither does He love us any less because we behave poorly. In other words, there is nothing we can do to lose God's love, and there is nothing we can do to gain it. People who truly understand the commitment of their Savior will seek to be more committed themselves.

Let's be committed to our husbands as our Savior is to us—forever.

Conclusion

*"Even as Sara obeyed Abraham,
calling him lord. . ." (I Peter 3:6)*

As I write this conclusion, I have finished studying the life of Sarah in my Bible. I read that God blessed Sarah and that He made her the mother of a great nation. I also read that Sarah was beautiful, even at ninety years of age. Yet, I find great imperfection and weakness in Sarah's life. She seems to have been a typical woman.

She exaggerated the truth sometimes. She told Abimelech that Abraham was her brother. Abraham was her half-brother, but Sarah failed to mention that he was also her husband.

Sarah was jealous. She sounds like a pretty typical woman to me. She asked Abraham to kick Hagar and Ishmael out of the house because she didn't want Ishmael to be heir with Isaac.

Sarah lacked great faith. She laughed at God's promise that she would have a son in her old age, and then she denied that she had done so. Genesis 18:12 says, *"Therefore Sarah laughed within herself, saying, After I am waxed old shall I have pleasure, my lord being old also."*

Sarah was self-willed. When she thought God had taken too long in keeping His promise to her, she decided to get what she wanted in her own time and in her own way. Perhaps if she had lived today, she would have charged things on her credit card that she couldn't afford because she didn't believe God would give her what she needed. Again, she sounds typical to me.

The only thing I can find about Sarah that might hint as to why she was used of God was her willingness to follow her husband. She left her homeland to follow Abraham and there is record of Sarah doing what Abraham told her to do several other times in Genesis. I have written this book on marriage principles because I believe that following one's husband is perhaps the greatest way to receive God's blessing.

In closing, I would also like to say that one of the greatest principles I have learned from the life of Sarah is that God uses typical women. In other words, God did not use Sarah because of Sarah; He used and blessed Sarah because of God and His Own greatness.

My prayer is that the marriage principles taught in this book will help other marriages as they have helped mine. If that happens, I believe the work of God will prosper more than it would have otherwise. My prayer also and especially is that those who read this book will remember that if God does bless or use your marriage or mine, it will not be because of this book or because of you or me. It will be because of God and His Own greatness.

"Unto him be glory in the church by Christ Jesus throughout all ages, world without end. Amen."
(Ephesians 5:21)